T0207348

Communications
in Computer and Information Science   1884

Rationale

The CCIS series is devoted to the publication of proceedings of computer science conferences. Its aim is to efficiently disseminate original research results in informatics in printed and electronic form. While the focus is on publication of peer-reviewed full papers presenting mature work, inclusion of reviewed short papers reporting on work in progress is welcome, too. Besides globally relevant meetings with internationally representative program committees guaranteeing a strict peer-reviewing and paper selection process, conferences run by societies or of high regional or national relevance are also considered for publication.

Topics

The topical scope of CCIS spans the entire spectrum of informatics ranging from foundational topics in the theory of computing to information and communications science and technology and a broad variety of interdisciplinary application fields.

Information for Volume Editors and Authors

Publication in CCIS is free of charge. No royalties are paid, however, we offer registered conference participants temporary free access to the online version of the conference proceedings on SpringerLink (http://link.springer.com) by means of an http referrer from the conference website and/or a number of complimentary printed copies, as specified in the official acceptance email of the event.

CCIS proceedings can be published in time for distribution at conferences or as post-proceedings, and delivered in the form of printed books and/or electronically as USBs and/or e-content licenses for accessing proceedings at SpringerLink. Furthermore, CCIS proceedings are included in the CCIS electronic book series hosted in the SpringerLink digital library at http://link.springer.com/bookseries/7899. Conferences publishing in CCIS are allowed to use Online Conference Service (OCS) for managing the whole proceedings lifecycle (from submission and reviewing to preparing for publication) free of charge.

Publication process

The language of publication is exclusively English. Authors publishing in CCIS have to sign the Springer CCIS copyright transfer form, however, they are free to use their material published in CCIS for substantially changed, more elaborate subsequent publications elsewhere. For the preparation of the camera-ready papers/files, authors have to strictly adhere to the Springer CCIS Authors' Instructions and are strongly encouraged to use the CCIS LaTeX style files or templates.

Abstracting/Indexing

CCIS is abstracted/indexed in DBLP, Google Scholar, EI-Compendex, Mathematical Reviews, SCImago, Scopus. CCIS volumes are also submitted for the inclusion in ISI Proceedings.

How to start

To start the evaluation of your proposal for inclusion in the CCIS series, please send an e-mail to ccis@springer.com.

Habtamu Abie · Vasileios Gkioulos ·
Sokratis Katsikas · Sandeep Pirbhulal
Editors

Secure and Resilient Digital Transformation of Healthcare

First Workshop, SUNRISE 2023
Stavanger, Norway, November 30, 2023
Proceedings

Springer

Editors
Habtamu Abie
Norwegian Computing Center
Oslo, Norway

Vasileios Gkioulos
Norwegian University of Science
and Technology
Gjøvik, Norway

Sokratis Katsikas
Norwegian University of Science
and Technology
Gjøvik, Norway

Sandeep Pirbhulal
Norwegian Computing Center
Oslo, Norway

ISSN 1865-0929   ISSN 1865-0937 (electronic)
Communications in Computer and Information Science
ISBN 978-3-031-55828-3   ISBN 978-3-031-55829-0 (eBook)
https://doi.org/10.1007/978-3-031-55829-0

This Springer imprint is published by the registered company Springer Nature Switzerland AG
The registered company address is: Gewerbestrasse 11, 6330 Cham, Switzerland

Paper in this product is recyclable.

Preface

SUNRISE 2023 is a forum for researchers and practitioners working on the secure and resilient digital transformation of healthcare. Digital transformation in healthcare encompasses the use of advanced technologies to enhance patient care and address the evolving demands of care delivery, particularly the transition to home-based care from hospital settings. While centering on patient needs, it also entails indispensable adjustments and advancements of healthcare processes. Whereas various benefits of this transformation are broadly acknowledged, the increased connectivity; the huge *volume of sensitive health information*; and the lack of sufficient cybersecurity awareness and culture among both healthcare professionals and patients result in increased cybersecurity risk and make digital healthcare attractive to cyber criminals and prone to cybersecurity attacks such as phishing, ransomware, distributed denial-of-service attacks, and malware. The connection of medical devices to the Internet, hospital networks, and other devices extends the potential for attacks, thereby raising concerns for patient safety. The COVID-19 pandemic brought attention to the interconnected nature of cybersecurity and privacy risks in healthcare. The need to enhance cybersecurity and resilience in healthcare and its supply chain has been heightened, requiring the development of new solutions.

To address these challenges, the workshop aimed to bring together security researchers and practitioners, healthcare professionals and managers of healthcare and rethink secure digitalization and resilience of healthcare.

The workshop garnered the attention of healthcare research communities and fostered novel insights and advancements, with a specific focus on cybersecurity skills, access control, privacy risks, and resilience within healthcare systems. The 1st Workshop on Secure and Resilient Digital Transformation of Healthcare (SUNRISE) 2023 was held in person. The workshop was organized in conjunction with the 35th Norwegian ICT Conference for Research and Education (NIKT 2023), 27–30 November 2023, University of Stavanger, Norway. The workshop consisted of two keynote addresses and technical presentations, with an attendance of approximately 20 individuals.

A total of nine submissions were received by the workshop, all of which were subsequently sent for reviews. As a result of an extensive peer-review process, four papers were selected to be presented at the workshop. The review process primarily emphasized the quality, scientific novelty, and applicability of the papers to safeguarding critical healthcare infrastructure and services. The acceptance rate stood at 50%. The accepted articles encompass a diverse range of techniques addressing cybersecurity skills, access control, privacy risks, and resilience in healthcare systems. The workshop showcased two significant and thought-provoking keynotes on the topics of "Healthcare 4.0: Data Analytics, Digital Transformation, and Cyber Security Perspective" and "Methodology for Automating Attacking Agents in Cyber Range Training Platforms," which were followed by the technical presentations.

The workshop was supported by the International Alliance for Strengthening Cybersecurity and Privacy in Healthcare (CybAlliance) project, the Center for Research-based

Innovation (SFI) Norwegian Center for Cybersecurity in Critical Sectors (NORCICS) project, and the AI-Based Scenario Management for Cyber Range Training (ASCERT) project. The organizers would like to thank these projects for supporting the SUNRISE 2023 workshop.

The organizers of the SUNRISE 2023 workshop would like to extend their heartfelt appreciation to the SUNRISE 2023 Program Committee for their meticulous and punctual review process, which played a crucial role in bringing the workshop to fruition. We would like to express our gratitude to the University of Stavanger, Norway for graciously hosting the workshop, and extend our appreciation to the NIKT 2023 chairs for their invaluable assistance and support.

December 2023   Habtamu Abie
                                                        Vasileios Gkioulos
                                                        Sokratis Katsikas
                                                        Sandeep Pirbhulal

Organization

Program Committee Chairs

Habtamu Abie	Norwegian Computing Center, Norway
Vasileios Gkioulos	Norwegian University of Science and Technology, Norway
Sokratis Katsikas	Norwegian University of Science and Technology, Norway
Sandeep Pirbhulal	Norwegian Computing Center, Oslo, Norway

Program Committee

Dieter Gollmann	Hamburg University of Technology, Germany
Joaquin Garcia-Alfaro	Télécom SudParis, France
Shouhuai Xu	University of Colorado, Colorado Springs, USA
Kai Rannenberg	Goethe University Frankfurt, Germany
Ilangko Balasingham	Oslo University Hospital, Norway
Maryline Laurent	Télécom SudParis, France
Nesrin Kaaniche	Télécom SudParis, France
Cristina Alcaraz	University of Malaga, Spain
Martin Gilje Jaatun	University of Stavanger, Norway
Audun Stolpe	Norwegian Computing Center, Norway
Mauro Conti	University of Padua, Italy
Fabio Martinelli	IIT-CNR, Italy
Christos Xenakis	University of Piraeus, Greece
Mohsen Toorani	University of South-Eastern Norway, Norway
Aida Omerovic	SINTEF, Norway
Hervé Debar	Télécom SudParis, France
Manos Athanatos	Foundation for Research and Technology Hellas, Crete
Sofia Tsekeridou	INTRASOFT International, Greece
Ilias Gkotsis	Satways Ltd., Greece
Isabel Praça	GECAD/ISEP, Portugal
Aida Akbarzadeh	Norwegian University of Science and Technology, Norway
Maria Tsirigoti	Institute of Communication and Computer Systems, Greece

Laidi Roufaida   Norwegian University of Science and Technology,
                                    Norway
Ali Dehghantanha   University of Guelph, Canada
Vasileios Mavroeidis   University of Oslo, Norway
Reijo Savola   University of Jyväskylä, Finland

External Reviewers

Wolfgang Leister   Norwegian Computing Center, Norway
Ankur Shukla   Institute for Energy Technology, Norway
Michail Bampatsikos   University of Piraeus, Greece
Ekzhin Ear   University of Colorado, Colorado Springs, USA
Sabarathinam Chockalingam   Institute for Energy Technology, Norway
Georgios Kavallieratos   Norwegian University of Science and Technology,
                                    Norway

Contents

Contents

Cybersecurity Skills and Access Control in Healthcare

Training on Social Media Cybersecurity Skills in the Healthcare Context

Mario Fernandez-Tarraga[1] , Alejandro-David Cayuela-Tudela[1] ,

Pantaleone Nespoli[1,2(✉)] , Joaquin Garcia-Alfaro[2] , and Félix Gómez Mármol[1]

[1] Departamento de Ingeniería de la Información y las Comunicaciones, Universidad de Murcia, 30100 Murcia, Spain
{mario.fernandezt,alejandrodavid.cayuelat,
pantaleone.nespoli,felixgm}@um.es

[2] SAMOVAR, Télécom SudParis, Institut Polytechnique de Paris, 19 place Marguerite Perey, 91120 Palaiseau, France
{pantaleone.nespoli,joaquin.garcia_alfaro}@telecom-sudparis.eu

Abstract. In the last decades, social media has experienced exponential growth due to its popularity and advantages in communication, connection, and broadcasting, etc. Nevertheless, social media also presents disadvantages and threats that can be exploited for evil ends. Indeed, it has become a vector of attack for cybercriminals and scammers. Broadcasting and public access have allowed the public to post fake news and disinformation. The wrong use of social media by users due to negligence or unawareness allows these threats to succeed. In this scenario, the healthcare sector is also affected by social media threats, as can be seen over the years in the frequent daily phishing attacks, vulnerable devices, data leaks of personal information, etc. This article proposes an automated tool for training social media cybersecurity competencies in the social and professional sectors of the healthcare environment, built on the Cyber Range context. It allows automating the generation and configuration of simulated social media exercises with several levels of content, difficulty, and realism, creating multiple hyperrealistic situations across a wide range of possibilities. Training phishing attacks, crisis management, social media attacks, and pandemic or disease crisis disinformation are some of the possibilities, both theoretical and practical.

Keywords: Cyber Range · Cybersecurity · Cyberdefense · Social media simulation · Social media cybersecurity skills · Digital education · E-health · Digital health · Healthcare cybersecurity

1 Introduction

Since the second half of the 20th century, technology has evolved exponentially, culminating in the present technological and digital state. One of the main exponents of such an evolution is social media, whose hyperconnectivity has facilitated the globalisation of information and communication with thousands of people, among many other advantages [5]. Even with the daily use of social media, not all users are aware of the disadvantages and threats posed by the use of these platforms, where different actors with malicious objectives participate directly or indirectly.

© The Author(s), under exclusive license to Springer Nature Switzerland AG 2024
H. Abie et al. (Eds.): SUNRISE 2023, CCIS 1884, pp. 3–20, 2024.
https://doi.org/10.1007/978-3-031-55829-0_1

Technological evolution affects society in all areas. The transformation of sectors such as healthcare towards a more digitalised environment has led to the widespread use of the internet, making social media and other online services indispensable. Consequently, healthcare is also vulnerable to various threats associated with internet and social media usage. The study conducted by the European Network and Information Security Agency (ENISA) [6] outlines cybersecurity threats within healthcare environments, many of which are connected to or stem from social media.

On the one hand, there are problems related to communication and interaction between patients and professionals on social media, as well as threats related to privacy and security [4], the influence of social bots and their dangers [15], threats related to disinformation or misinformation in the medical field [10]. Not to mention the use of social media in managing potential social and health crises such as the COVID-19 pandemic [8]. On the other hand, social media enables both gathering information to prepare more elaborate attacks and attacking vulnerable users with social engineering, phishing, OSINT techniques [14] or uploading malware. Phishing is a common attack in this area, with high success rates, including within hospital environments [18]. The majority of successful attempts can be attributed to user distractions and negligence, since many attacks are recognisable with awareness. The gravest consequences, such as data breaches, can result in catastrophic losses, both in terms of patients' personal information and the loss of essential patient diagnostics and records necessary for providing continuous, essential services [19]. Ultimately, many of these challenges converge on the vulnerability of the human factor in the cybersecurity chain, as underscored by numerous studies [3,7,9,12].

This article proposes an automated tool for social and professional training to mitigate the aforementioned challenges, building upon the structure of well-known Cyber Ranges [16], through an automated social media training system. This proposal holds immense importance, especially in the healthcare context, where training and knowledge can make good habits and reduce cybersecurity incidents [21]. This training proposal toggles with the architecture required for its implementation and its automation. It allows for the easy setup and control of cyberexercises by automating their creation, execution, and adaptation to extensible, multidisciplinary, and hyperrealistic challenges.

The article is structured as follows: Sect. 2 shows the lack of academic work. Then, Sect. 3 explains the social media simulator proposed and its architecture. Next, Sect. 4 shows the general implementation of the proposal. Then, Sect. 5 displays an example of provisioning a basic exercise within the social media platform. Finally, Sect. 6 outlines the drawn conclusions and future work for this proposal.

2   State of the Art

Social simulation does not represent a novel idea in the literature and has been extensively explored in various studies focusing on behaviour, polarization, topic-centered communities, relationships between simulated agents, and more [1]. However, the specific simulation of social media platforms, especially concerning competency training in cybersecurity, remains a relatively unexplored domain. In other words, there is a frightening lack of tools that simulate social media scenarios to train competencies of cybersecurity. Furthermore, the few solutions are limited or specific approaches, and most of the solutions are developed by private companies, leaving little research in academia. The following paragraphs analyse the main solutions found in the literature, showing their main characteristics and comparisons.

The master's thesis [2] (CYRAN Cyber Range Extension) uses the first versions of open source social media platforms, with major limitations in functionality. These are the impossibility of using multimedia content and the automation of user creation, as well as the configuration of user profiles. The publication of content is done through pregenerated posts and dynamically generated (autogenerated) posts, which are published automatically according to the parameters entered in the templates for exercise generation. In this sense, exercises can be configured manually using these templates, but there are no mechanisms to automate the exercise creation process. In addition, the tool does not support hot configuration and settings, and does not allow multiple runs to be controlled simultaneously. However, the tool is designed to support several real users or students simultaneously and concurrently.

Another project [13] (Somulator) is developed by the Norwegian Defence Research Establishment (FFI) and by the Norwegian University of Science and Technology (NTNU), supports multimedia content, and allows the creation and configuration of users, automating only the creation processes. The publications used are pregenerated and loaded with templates. It does not allow the configuration of statistics, but it does allow the configuration of exercises (and also during the execution). The tool uses several open source platforms and is designed to be used simultaneously by many real users or students. In addition, it is complex to control several instances in parallel.

Besides, the third software service [17] (Prevency) also supports multimedia content and allows users to be created both individually and collectively by automating this process. The configuration of users and profiles can also be done both individually and automatically when creating such collective profiles. Publications are pregenerated and must be published deliberately. Additionally, it allows the configuration of statistics for both users and publications and permits hot settings. The tool is intended for use with several real users simultaneously; however, like its counterparts, it is not aimed at deploying an exercise across various individual instances (parallel control).

Table 1 shows the main differences according to the features of each proposal or tool, as well as their comparison with the proposal in this article. In particular, the last lines of the table show the new concepts explained in Sect. 3.1, which have not been explored by any of the previous proposals. In the following list, the meaning of each of the entries in the table previously mentioned is described:

- **Multimedia content**: The solution is not limited to text only, but also allows the use of multimedia content.
- **User creation**: The tool enables user manual creation and generation for the exercise within the platform.
- **User creation automation**: The tool automates the user creation process, both individual and collective creation.

Table 1. State of the art - Feature comparison.

Features	CYRAN	Somulator	Prevency	Proposal
Multimedia content	✗	✓	✓	✓
User creation	✓	✓	✓	✓
User creation automation	✗	✓	✓	✓
User configuration	✗	✓	✓	✓
User auto-configuration	✗	✗	✓	✓
Pregenerated content	✓	✓	✓	✓
Self-published	✓	✓	✗	✓
Exercise configuration	✓	✓	✓	✓
Exercise automation	✗	✗	✗	✓
Hot configuration	✗	✓	✓	✓
Real platforms	✓	✓	✗	✓
Parallel control	✗	✗	✗	✓
Multiple simultaneous users	✓	✓	✓	✓
Psychological profiles	✗	✗	✗	✓
Behavior profiles	✗	✗	✗	✓
User relationships	✗	✗	✗	✓

- **User configuration**: The configuration of the profiles, advanced options, and privacy of the created users is contemplated.
- **User auto-configuration**: The created users can be auto-configured automatically by the tool.
- **Pregenerated content**: The solution allows the creation and configuration of publications and contents, which can be used during the execution of the cyberexercise.
- **Self-published**: Assigned content can be published automatically, either by pre-scheduling or dynamic publishing, without the need for direct human intervention.
- **Exercise configuration**: Exercises can be created and configured manually, adding users, publications, and other elements according to the requirements.
- **Exercise automation**: The process of creating social media exercises is fully or partially automated.
- **Hot configuration**: The exercise configuration can be modified while the exercise is running, adding or modifying elements such as users and publications.
- **Real platforms**: The solution uses existing social media platforms as the basis, not those specifically designed from scratch that are a software product rather than a social media platform.
- **Parallel control**: The tool is designed to monitor and manage multiple instances of the same social media exercise simultaneously.
- **Multiple simultaneous users**: Several users can connect to the same instance and operate at the same time.
- **Psychological profiles**: Psychological descriptions can be set up on users, allowing them to interpret incoming content and generate content based on their preferences.

– **Behaviour profiles**: Specific actions and behaviours can be configured for specific situations and events, such as publishing content, replying to publications and mentions, updating relationships, etc.
– **User relationships**: Basic relationships and connections between users created in social media can be configured, such as follow, block, mute, etc.

3   Proposal

This section outlines the article's proposal within the context of social media simulation exercises for cybercompetencies training. Concretely, a cybercompetency is a skill related to the secure use of social media platforms and the internet. Section 3.1 presents the social media training simulator and Sect. 3.2 its corresponding architecture.

3.1   Social Media Training Simulator

The proposal is centred around a tool that automates the process of creating and provisioning simulated cyberexercises in social media within the Cyber Range context and their advanced configuration. According to NIST a Cyber Range is an interactive platform to simulate all types of cybersecurity scenarios with their components with simulations of internet traffic or services. This virtualisation platform provides the opportunity to present and use a secure, controlled and legal environment to develop cybersecurity skills [16]. Typically, the structure of a Cyber Range is a composition of a user interface based on front-end technologies, the features that the Cyber Range can deploy or that are available (virtualisation, monitoring, simulation of services and internet, etc.) and finally, the Cyber Range infrastructure itself managed by the orchestrator (proper virtualisation, containerisation, emulation and simulation) [20]. Thus, the Cyber Range environment enables the generation of hyperrealistic simulations for cybercompetencies training in any scenario or situation, qualifying various social stratum and professional sectors against imminent threats and risks caused by, related to, or developed in social media. The training is carried out by three roles: students who perform the social media cyberexercise, instructors who design, prepare, and build the cyberexercise, and administrators who manage the Cyber Range. It is worth noting that automation is a crucial and fundamental new feature of the proposal. It facilitates the effortless, swift, and efficient generation of training, thereby fostering the development of competencies with minimal effort.

The proposed solution utilises open source social media platforms, concretely Mastodon[1], which serves as an alternative to Twitter. It is a social media platform based on microblogging similar to Twitter (now known as X), and the decision to use Mastodon for social media simulation is based on the advantages and features it offers, as well as the current social context, adapting perfectly to the needs and objectives of the proposal. The main advantages are its open source code, the number of libraries and functionalities it offers to build the necessary modules and functions, as well as its easy installation, configuration, and deployment. Also, the most valuable feature is

---

[1] https://docs.joinmastodon.org/.

the automation capability for creating and configuring users, including the ability to skip authentication steps for new users by using the platform's own internal administration commands. Furthermore, using a Twitter-like platform allows students to learn in a close-to-reality environment, enhancing the training.

The following new innovative concepts presented in this proposal, combined with the improved foundational concepts, facilitate advanced simulations with hyperrealistic scenarios for various contexts.

- **Personality**: It attributes psychological descriptions and preferences. Such a feature aids in the interpretation and classification of incoming content, and generating automatic responses and posts that are aligned with the simulated user personality.
- **Behaviour**: It provides simulated users with actions and interactions, enabling them to perform tasks such as posting, and responding to notifications. It also allows the configuration and generation of concrete reactions to specific events, differentiating between target users by user type or current relationship.
- **Relationships**: It establishes connections between users, allowing them to form and accept friendship requests, follow, block, or mute other users, and accept or decline follow requests.
- **Profile configuration**: It provides simulated users with profile and privacy settings. It is used to customise the simulated users' profiles with biographies, aliases, profile pictures, other privacy options, and other features.

Besides, several enhancements are proposed through process automation. These automations are achieved using superparameters and base templates. Templates used to generate exercises and the required configurations for provisioning the simulation. The templates or base templates are guides or JSON-format models containing elements with the configuration and provisioning of a simulation (see Sect. 4, Table 3), and superparameters are parameters used to determine the automated construction and configuration of a base template (see Table 2). Concretely, proposed automations include:

1. **Creation and configuration of social media cyberexercises**: The creation of cyberexercises is automated, allowing the instructor to obtain a usable, configured base template with a few easy-to-use superparameters, such as the type of exercise (disinformation, phishing, social engineering attacks, and more), the topic (COVID-19 pandemic, health crisis, and others.) or the number of simulated interactions.
2. **Advanced configuration of cyberexercises**: The basic templates generated can be configured at different levels of detail, with infinite possibilities thanks to the new concepts proposed. Thus, the configuration of specific user profiles, new relationships between users, specific complex actions, and much more are possible.
3. **Creation and customisation of users**: User creation is automated, distinguishing between relevant and random users, for example, the configuration of the novel concepts previously introduced (i.e. profiles, relationships, personalities, and behaviours) is automated.
4. **Cyberexercise content**: The generation of content and key publications necessary for the development of the cyberexercise is automated, and classified into types according to the topic, exercise type, or other superparameters. When creating base templates for a concrete exercise, compatible template elements are selected and

filtered by the specified superparameters. This way, choosing a disinformation exercise will return publications, users, personalities and behaviours needed to develop a disinformation exercise.

5. **Simulated Non Playable Character (NPC) content**: Interactions, content generation, and posts used as background traffic are automated to animate the simulation. An NPC could follow another user, post a photo, and more. In this way, a real user the social media is completely authentic with NPC users talking or posting.

In addition, it is relevant to note that the tool is designed to be integrated into a Cyber Range and therefore needs to be applied in multiple cyberexercises instances. Also, in particular, deployments of the same cyberexercise should be consistent for all students, with the base configuration being identical, differing only in the dynamic background traffic. This way, the training of multiple students can be easily controlled by varying unimportant background traffic while maintaining the key features of the cyberexercise. Similarly, the tool should allow the instructor to interact with the simulations during the cyberexercise, whether for individual or group deployments. The Hot Configuration will be explained in the Sect. 3.

3.2   Architecture

The proposed architecture is based on the typical structure of a Cyber Range, expanding upon the architecture proposed in the COBRA Cyber Range [11] to focus on the development of features for social media training modules. The tool's design, based on independent systems and modules from a specific Cyber Range, renders it exceedingly extensible and autonomous, despite reusing the architecture from the Cyber Range COBRA proposal. Figure 1 illustrates the proposed architecture, and the following sections describe and detail its components.

Front-End Architecture. It is an architecture based on Docker containers reused from COBRA. The Fig. 1 shows the systems to which the front-end should be connected. As a result of these connections with the managers, it is abstracted from the inclusion of new modules into the systems to raise the functionality, and it is very easy to change the front-end with other options.

Scenarios, Challenges and Cyberexercises Creation System. The objective of the Creation System is to provide the necessary configurations and capabilities to Virtual Machines (VMs) that will be used to carry out the training. Subsequently, the System will deploy the VMs, and configure the challenges and cyberexercises. A challenge is a task that students need to overcome. Moreover, the choice of features and parameters of social media, where the training is conducted, is determined here. A Cyberexercise is a series of one or more challenges that may or may not share the same training objective. Each instance of a Cyberexercise is referred to as a deployment. The configurations of virtual machines and social media platforms are carried out here.

Firstly, the front-end communicates with the Creation Manager, which handles the requests for the creation of scenarios, challenges, and cyberexercises. Secondly, the

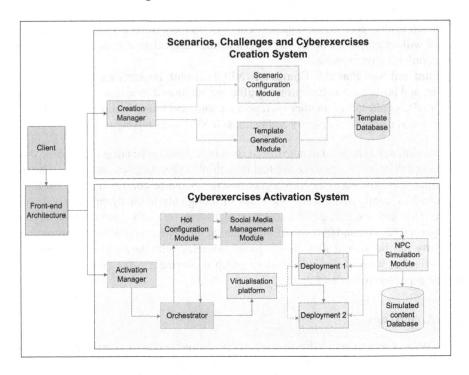

Fig. 1. Architecture of the social media simulator

manager forwards all information in the requests to the Scenario Configuration Module (SCM). Finally, it communicates with the Template Generation Module (TGM) to obtain the final challenge template.

The SCM is responsible for creating scenarios with one or multiple VMs. It is possible to configure parameters such as the operating system, services or applications, files that should be present on the machine, and the characteristics of the VM itself. To ensure the configuration is modular and extensible, services are implemented as *Docker* containers, and any type of file can be sent to the VMs. For social media, training is mandatory for at least one of the VMs to run the Mastodon service.

Following the scenario creation, the instructor proceeds to create and configure the challenge using superparameters explained in Sect. 4. The TGM will provide a JSON template containing the complete configuration of the challenge, including instructions for configuring the instance, which will be loaded into Mastodon after activation.

For generating templates, the TGM possesses a database with previous templates with social media content generated based on topics, kinds of training, objectives, and so forth. It also has configurations for personalities and behaviours, automation for user parameterisation and deployment, number of posts and much more.

Cyberexercises Activation System. The Activation System is designed to guarantee suitable deployment, activation, and execution of cyberexercises. Either an instructor or student of the training user can access this system. Similar to the Creation Manager, the front-end communicates with the Activation Manager, which handles requests and allows the activation/deactivation of cyberexercises. Furthermore, it enables the connection between the student and the virtual environment where the training will take place.

On the one hand, if access is granted with the instructor role, it is possible to start the cyberexercise. The orchestrator automates processes related to virtual machine creation and management, and performs communication and management tasks for different modules within the cyber range. It requests the virtualization platform to deploy the VMs and provisions them with the needed operating system and services, such as Mastodon. Once the deployment is successful, the orchestrator contacts the Hot Configuration Module to send the cyberexercise base template to prepare the initial state of the challenge.

It is worth noting that each deployment has its Social Media Management Module (SMMM) and NPC Simulation Module, which run locally in the VM where Mastodon is located. The SMMM module is responsible for ensuring that the training can be carried out. The SMMM module guarantees the execution of cyberexercises, making it the foremost module with extensive functionality. Specifically, it updates and manages exercise information dynamically. The SMMM receives and analyses the template, generates the configuration, and loads it into the local Mastodon instance. Once loaded, it continues to monitor the health of the social media platform.

On the other hand, if a student accesses, it could connect to the VMs via remote desktop applications. Once connected to the VM, the student can start the cyberexercise to train, and, thus develop the competencies specified by the instructor. This cyberexercise can be conducted for the duration specified in the configuration file.

Additionally, the NPC simulation module is employed to bring to life the social media simulation. This module generates simulated traffic, meaning that it creates and publishes content related to the personalities of the NPCs, and creates interactions among simulation users. Similarly to the database in the Template Generation module, the NPC simulation module also possesses a database with previously generated content. This database is accessed by the NPC simulation module to generate automatically responses or publications made by the NPC users using the pregenerated content based on their personality, behaviour and desired topic.

4   Implementation

This section explores the general implementation of the proposal, following the processes previously described from the creation of scenarios and challenges, the activation of a cyberexercise and its execution. These processes include the modules discussed in Sect. 3, whose functionalities allow automating and simplifying the proceedings of generation and configuration of the social media platform instances to generate more efficient, effective and realistic cyberexercises.

The following subsections explain the modules used in the proposal. Subsection 4.1 details the template generation module, which automates the creation of social media exercises, while Subsect. 4.2 shows the Social Media Management Module. Then, in

Table 2. Superparameter description.

Superparameter	Definition	Objective	Required	Dependencies	Values
Topic	Main theme of the exercise used for relevant content	Generate a themed template for the exercise.	✗	✗	Text
Type	Type of exercise or use case to be generated	Generate a base template for a specific use case	✓	✗	Use case
Subtype	Subtype of exercise or specific use case to be generated	Generate a base template for the implementation of a specific use case	✗	Type	Specific use case
Users amount	Simulated users amount	Generate a random users amount	✗	✗	Positive integer
Simulated traffic	Simulated traffic frequency and amount	Configure the amount and frequency of interactions generated by NPC	✗	✗	Percentage
Topic divergence	Divergence between simulated traffic topic and main topic	Configure the emergence of topics separate from the main topic	✗	✗	Percentage
User divergence	Divergence between user behaviour and user personality	Generate users with different behaviour and personality	✗	✗	Percentage
Configuration level	Automatic template configuration	Generate templates at various configuration levels	✗	✗	Percentage
Bot amount	Percentage of automated bots	Generate a percentage of bot accounts	✗	Automation level	Percentage
Automation level	Humanity of bots	Configure bot humanity level	✗	Bot amount	Percentage

Subsect. 4.3, the Hot Configuration Module is explained, and finally, in Subsect. 4.4, the NPC Simulation Module is described.

4.1   Template Generation Module

The first step is to generate and configure a base template (as described in Sect. 3.1), which will be used to provision the social media instances. These templates are typically generated manually, but such a procedure requires extensive knowledge of the tool due to the extensive configuration possibilities. To simplify and automate this creation process, the Template Generation Module is provided, enabling the template generation by using a few superparameters, as explained in Sect. 3.1. This module consists of a database that maintains fragments of templates and permits the generation of a base template according to these superparameters (used as filters). Table 2 shows the superparameters, their definition, their use, whether they are required or mandatory, the dependencies between other superparameters, and the value that must be assigned (e.g. the superparameter *type* refers to filter of the type of exercise required, such as a disinformation exercise, a phishing scenario, etc., used to classify and retrieve compatible template elements. The superparameter is always required, it has no dependencies on other superparameters, and valid values are the defined exercise types in the filter).

Based on the superparameters chosen by the instructor, the cyberexercise TGM retrieves automatically all compatible fragments from the database, and then it builds the base template by adapting it to the specifications, automating the process. The recurring elements of a base template are displayed in Table 3, together with their description and usage (e.g. the template element *publications* is a JSON entry list of publications, where each publication has its content, used to create and schedule a user's pregenerated posts on the social media platform). These received templates must be reviewed by the instructor, who will decide if it is valid or if they must be manually modified for the cyberexercise (Sect. 3.2).

4.2   Social Media Management Module (SMMM)

Once the cyberexercise is activated, the templates configured by the instructor are sent and loaded into the selected deployments within the virtual environment. The SMMM receives and maps the templates to objects that store and work with the information provided. It also executes the necessary actions and procedures to provide the social media instances with the template configurations and update the information for its internal management.

The procedure followed when loading a template is divided into two phases. The first phase consists of receiving and processing the base template, traversing it and its elements to convert it into objects. Behaviour and personality lists are loaded, and relevant and random users are assigned. In the second phase, all User objects are traversed, and the simulation is provisioned with the assigned configuration. The provisioning process in the second phase is divided into several stages:

1. **User creation and profile configuration**: Users are created and individual sessions with the social media platform are generated. Profiles are then configured.

Table 3. Template elements.

Template element	Definition	Use
Predefined templates	Previously created base templates	Loads pre-existing configured exercise base templates
Random users	Configurations for user creation	Set up and create different numbers of NPC users with common characteristics
Relevant users	Configurations for relevant user creation	Set up and create users configured with the given characteristics
Profile configuration	Specific profile configuration for users	Set up users profile configuration
Relationships	Configurations for user relationships	Set up base relationships as add, block, mute requests
Publications	List of user publications with assigned content	Create pregenerated publications and post them
Behaviour	Permitted action configuration	Set up user actions and behaviours for publishing content and interact
Behaviour functions	NPC authorised actions	Set up NPC user actions
Personality	User psychological description	Set up user personality for interpretation and content generation

2. **Relationship generation**: For each user follow, mute, block and other requests are made. Then, for each user again, received requests are accepted or rejected, updating the current relationships.
3. **Content publication**: For each user assigned pregenerated publications are sent.
4. **User simulation**: For each user, a thread is created to run the simulated traffic, based on the user's personality and behaviour. The execution of these threads is included in the NPC Simulation Module.

4.3 Hot Configuration Module

While the cyberexercise is running and deployments are operational, it may be necessary to make changes to these instances, for which we need a hot configuration module. This module facilitates modifying the running social media simulations. To achieve this, several mechanisms must be developed to enable the addition of new elements through the use of templates (new personalities, behaviours, users, and publications or content). These additions can be applied to specific or grouped deployments. Furthermore, the module should provide control actions that can be sent to influence these simulations. Some control actions can go directly to social network functioning, background traffic, NPC or relevant users, etc.

4.4 NPC Simulation Module

This module permits simulating users their personalities and their assigned behaviours. Specifically, personalities dictate the user's *personality*, determine how the simulated users will interpret a particular message, comment or topic, and respond based on their tastes and interests (whether they agree or disagree, if they insult, support, etc.). Then, behaviours dictate the actions they can take to generate background traffic, such as replies to public content, private notifications, etc.

The module consists of running threads for each user, which perform a looping process, selecting actions by categories according to the functionality required in the behaviour. Firstly, the publication actions are performed, both public and private. Then the actions related to the notifications received are performed. Next, the public publications are processed, and finally, the control and internal update actions are executed.

5 Demo

This section shows the result of provisioning a template to demonstrate that the proposal can automate the deployment of a social media exercise, as well as the interactions and actions that can be performed by simulated users within the platform.

In this template, three relevant manually configured users (*DrSigmunFraud, DefinitelyNotAHacker, and Fake News Channel*) and six other random autoconfigured users (they will be autoconfigured as *Samuel29, emorris, michaelmiller, zacharyperry, wcole, jessicaalexander*) are declared. Particularly, several behaviours and personalities are also configured to enable the autoconfigured users to generate automatic actions within the platform, such as replying to new messages, boosting posts, adding them to favourites, following users etc. Moreover, some users have declared predefined publications and relationships with other users.

Firstly, Fig. 2 presents the creation of the three manually configured users (*DrSigmunFraud, DefinitelyNotAHacker, and Fake News Channel*), who have been provided with profile pictures, descriptions, publications, and relationships manually.

Fig. 2. Relevant users generation.

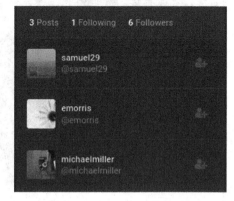

Fig. 3. Creating relationships

Secondly, Fig. 3 reveals some generated relationships, where *samuel29, emorris, and michaelmiller* and some users follow the shown account (*Fake News Channel*). In addition, the behaviour declared in the template may also generate follow, block, or mute relationships.

Then, Fig. 4 displays the self-configured random creation of six users, resulting in realistic profiles of a social media platform, while Fig. 5 reveals an autoconfigured user profile (*samuel29*) showing various user statistics. These statistics are related to the assigned behaviour, as it allows replying to posts, marking them as favourites, following other users, etc., automatically. The figure highlights its profile images, biography, boosted posts, replies, and followed users.

Fig. 4. Random user generation.   **Fig. 5.** User interactions.

Finally, Fig. 6 illustrates some responses and interactions of a disinformation fake new about COVID-19, which could be part of a disinformation campaign. Here it is possible to observe those user behaviours that have generated several responses to a posting event of another user they follow. Moreover, if we look at the responses of users jessicaalexander and zacharyperry, a more complex response action can be observed, which corresponds to a mention to the original user of the post.

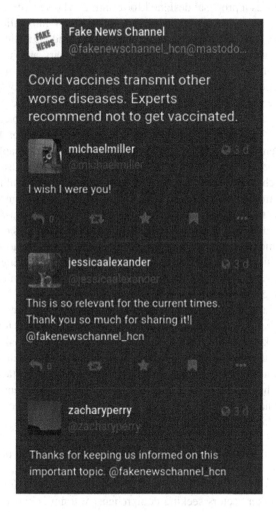

Fig. 6. Behaviour actions and replies.

To sum up, with this demo, it is shortly demonstrated that the proposal of this article can generate both concrete users manually and random users, individually or collectively, in an automatic way. Then, the setup of posts enables the design and advancement of particular cyberexercises. The utilization of specific behaviors or actions enhances the realism and functionality of the social media platform, enabling the creation of highly realistic exercises and scenarios. This, in turn, facilitates the training of cybersecurity competencies within social media platforms.

6   Conclusions and Future Work

This article introduces a proposal designed for training cybersecurity competencies on social media platforms. The proposed tool is prepared for integration into a Cyber Range. Specifically, this tool aims to make the training and education of professionals more efficient, achieving this by presenting the necessary architecture for proper deployment and automation in generating and managing cyberexercises. Also, the Cyber Range framework allows for simulations of adaptable difficulty levels and learning objectives, catering to competencies, topics, and final goals. The proposal is flexible, providing the capability to generate highly configurable, extensible, and multidisciplinary challenges. This involves an automated simulation generation feature utilizing the foundational templates outlined in Sect. 4 as a basic or customisable element. Furthermore, the proposal introduces the option to incorporate NPC users with specific characteristics, such as the innovative concepts of behavior, personality, and relationships, adding functionality, depth and realism to the training environment.

To demonstrate the feasibility of the proposal, a demonstration showcasing its functionality is provided in Sect. 5. It illustrates the creation of two types of users, the publication of social media content, the generation and building of relationships between users, and the configurations and behaviors that contribute to making a social media platform realistic. Additionally, it highlights the automatic execution of actions essential for creating diverse cyberexercises.

Looking ahead to future work, there are several key areas of focus. These include exploring the integration of other open-source social media platforms to simulate highly known platforms like Facebook, YouTube, Telegram, etc., thereby making the proposal more versatile. Furthermore, it is proposed to design and create an automated module for dynamic content generation. This module would enable the obtaining of existing content and the generation of new content, aligned with the requirements of behavior and personality. Finally, there is a plan to develop a module for the collection and evaluation of student data, aiming to enhance the efficacy and adaptability of the training platform.

In conclusion, the ongoing development and expansion of the proposed training tool for cybersecurity competencies on social media platforms promise to bring about a more versatile, adaptive, and effective solution for professionals, organisations in the field of health or other sectors seeking comprehensive training experiences related to the social part of the internet.

Acknowledgements. This work has been partially funded by the Spanish Ministry of Universities linked to the European Union through the NextGenerationEU programme, from the post-doctoral grant Margarita Salas (172/MSJD/22). Authors acknowledge as well support from the CybAlliance project (Grant no. 337316).

References

1. Amblard, F., Bouadjio-Boulic, A., Gutiérrez, C.S., Gaudou, B.: Which models are used in social simulation to generate social networks? A review of 17 years of publications in jasss. In: 2015 Winter Simulation Conference (WSC), pp. 4021–4032. IEEE (2015)
2. Braidley, S.: Extending our cyber-range cyran with social engineering capabilities. Master's thesis. De Montfort University, Leicester, England (2016)
3. Colwill, C.: Human factors in information security: the insider threat-who can you trust these days? Inf. Secur. Tech. Rep. **14**(4), 186–196 (2009)
4. Denecke, K., et al.: Ethical issues of social media usage in healthcare. Yearb. Med. Inform. **24**(01), 137–147 (2015)
5. Drahošová, M., Balco, P.: The analysis of advantages and disadvantages of use of social media in European union. Procedia Comput. Sci. **109**, 1005–1009 (2017)
6. ENISA: Health Threat Landscape. Technical report, ENISA (2023). https://doi.org/10.2824/163953. https://www.enisa.europa.eu/publications/health-threat-landscape
7. Geeng, C., Yee, S., Roesner, F.: Fake news on facebook and twitter: investigating how people (don't) investigate. In: Proceedings of the 2020 CHI Conference on Human Factors in Computing Systems, pp. 1–14 (2020)
8. González-Padilla, D.A., Tortolero-Blanco, L.: Social media influence in the covid-19 pandemic. Int. Braz J Urol **46**, 120–124 (2020)
9. Hadlington, L.: Human factors in cybersecurity; examining the link between internet addiction, impulsivity, attitudes towards cybersecurity, and risky cybersecurity behaviours. Heliyon **3**(7), 18 (2017)
10. Naeem, S.B., Bhatti, R., Khan, A.: An exploration of how fake news is taking over social media and putting public health at risk. Health Inf. Libr. J. **38**(2), 143–149 (2021)
11. Nespoli, P., Albaladejo-González, M., Pastor Valera, J.A., Ruipérez-Valiente, J.A., Gómez Mármol, F.: Capacidades avanzadas de simulación y evaluación con elementos de gamificación. In: VII Jornadas Nacionales de Investigación en Ciberseguridad (JNIC 2022), pp. 55–62 (2022)
12. Nifakos, S., et al.: Influence of human factors on cyber security within healthcare organisations: a systematic review. Sensors **21**(15), 5119 (2021)
13. Norwegian University of Science and Technology, Norwegian Defense Research Establishment: Somulator. https://www.ntnu.no/ncr/somulator. https://www.ffi.no/forskning/prosjekter/somulator. Accessed 15 Sept 2023
14. Pastor-Galindo, J., Nespoli, P., Gómez Mármol, F., Martínez Pérez, G.: The not yet exploited goldmine of OSINT: opportunities, open challenges and future trends. IEEE Access **8**, 10282–10304 (2020). https://doi.org/10.1109/ACCESS.2020.2965257
15. Pastor-Galindo, J., et al.: Spotting political social bots in twitter: a use case of the 2019 Spanish general election. IEEE Trans. Netw. Serv. Manage. **17**(4), 2156–2170 (2020). https://doi.org/10.1109/TNSM.2020.3031573
16. Petersen, R., Santos, D., Smith, M.C., Wetzel, K.A., Witte, G.: Workforce framework for cybersecurity (NICE framework). Technical report, NIST (2020). https://nvlpubs.nist.gov/nistpubs/SpecialPublications/NIST.SP.800-181r1.pdf
17. Prevency: Project NATO Stratcom COE. https://prevency.com/en/projects/project-nato-stratcom-coe/. Accessed 15 Sept 2023
18. Rizzoni, F., Magalini, S., Casaroli, A., Mari, P., Dixon, M., Coventry, L.: Phishing simulation exercise in a large hospital: a case study. Digit. Health **8**, 20552076221081716 (2022). https://doi.org/10.1177/20552076221081716. pMID: 35321019
19. Seh, A.H., et al.: Healthcare data breaches: insights and implications. In: Healthcare, vol. 8, p. 133. MDPI (2020)

20. Ukwandu, E., et al.: A review of cyber-ranges and test-beds: current and future trends. Sensors **20**(24) (2020). https://doi.org/10.3390/s20247148. https://www.mdpi.com/1424-8220/20/24/7148
21. Zafar, H.: Cybersecurity: role of behavioral training in healthcare. In: Americas Conference on Information Systems (2016)

Blockchain-Based Access Control for Electronic Health Records

Khandoker Tahmid Sami$^{(\boxtimes)}$ and Mohsen Toorani$^{(\boxtimes)}$

Department of Science and Industry Systems, University of South-Eastern Norway,
Kongsberg, Norway
prinon96@gmail.com, mohsen.toorani@usn.no

Abstract. Blockchain-based access control mechanisms have the potential to significantly enhance the security and privacy of electronic health record systems. Electronic health data, vital for diagnosis, treatment, recovery, and medical accident investigation, must be protected to ensure its integrity and availability. This requires preserving the accuracy, reliability, and accessibility of this critical information within the healthcare ecosystem. Blockchain technology offers substantial potential for authenticating and preserving the integrity of access to electronic health data. In this paper, we propose a blockchain-based access control framework for electronic health record systems. This framework allows individuals to manage their digital identities in accordance with Self-Sovereign Identity (SSI) principles. It uses attribute-based access control (ABAC) to safeguard the privacy and security of electronic health data. The framework is designed to protect electronic health data during user access and employs Hyperledger Indy and Hyperledger Aries for sovereignty, with the Open Policy Agent (OPA) utilized for access control.

Keywords: Attribute-based Access Control · Self-Sovereign Identity · Hyperledger Indy · Hyperledger Aries · Open Policy Agent

1 Introduction

In the modern world, health is a universal concern. The healthcare sector is constantly evolving to meet these needs, with patient medical data at the heart of these changes. The protection of this sensitive data from potential threats is a critical requirement for today's advanced healthcare systems. To ensure that only authorized individuals can access a patient's medical information, it is vital to have secure data access procedures in place.

Blockchain technology could be a game-changer in managing medical records and other sensitive information. It offers Distributed Ledger Technology (DLT) that facilitates safe and secure transactions between two or more parties [8]. Currently, most medical and personal data are stored by hospitals or doctors' offices, resembling a centralized system. However, several challenges are associated with such a system [24, 26]:

H. Abie et al. (Eds.): SUNRISE 2023, CCIS 1884, pp. 21–33, 2024.
https://doi.org/10.1007/978-3-031-55829-0_2

- **Single point of failure:** All information is stored in one place or organization in a centralized system. Any disruption or failure could lead to loss of data access or total system failure.
- **Limited user control:** Users may have limited or no control over their data in a centralized system. This can potentially infringe the user privacy.
- **Scalability challenges:** Centralized systems may face difficulties when scaling up to meet increasing demands or user numbers. Performance issues may arise due to the concentration of all activities and data in one place.
- **Security risks:** Centralized systems are attractive targets for cyber attacks due to the possibility of gaining access to all data and control through a successful breach. This can lead to data breaches, identity theft, and other security risks.
- **Unavailability:** Centralized systems may face availability threats, including Denial-of-Service (DoS) attacks that can make the system unavailable to users. In emergency cases where medical data needs to be accessed urgently, such unavailability can have severe consequences and pose a risk to patient health and safety.

An electronic health record (EHR) is a digital version of a patient's health record that includes highly sensitive private information on history, diagnosis, and treatment. Other stored EHR data typically include appointments, billing details, and laboratory tests [12]. A centralized EHR is vulnerable to cyber attacks, which could compromise its security and privacy [17]. Blockchain technology can be beneficial in such scenarios due to its ability to create secure, transparent, and decentralized systems [12,20].

Blockchain technology has emerged as an important tool for managing, storing, and sharing data across various industries [15]. It has the potential to transform how medical data is accessed and managed by enhancing the availability of patient health data through decentralization. By integrating various access control policies with blockchain technology, the capabilities of existing blockchain-based systems can be expanded beyond their current limitations. By focusing on specific use cases such as medical data, this research could have a direct impact on healthcare systems, benefiting society at large.

SSI is an emerging technology that gives individuals full control over their digital identities [16,25]. It is crucial for EHRs because it provides privacy, security, efficiency, and empowerment of individuals. With SSI, users can control their data, protect against identity theft, streamline verification processes, and empower themselves by having control over their health data [13].

In this paper, we introduce a framework for blockchain-based access control for electronic health records. It will enable individuals to assert control over their digital identities using the principles of SSI. It ensures the privacy and security of medical health records using ABAC and protects medical data during user access. Its development is based on Hyperledger Indy and Hyperledger Aries to establish self-sovereignty, with the utilization of OPA for access control. In this paper, we only consider the access control. We do not go through the sharing of information or data storage. This could be done using a number of techniques, e.g., using InterPlanetary File System (IPFS) [5]. The remainder of this paper is organized as follows. The proposed framework is presented in Sect. 2, related work is discussed in Sect. 3, and Sect. 4 concludes the paper.

2   Proposed Framework

In this section, we introduce a framework designed to address the challenges associated with securing and managing access to medical health records. This is achieved by integrating the principles of SSI and ABAC with blockchain technology. The proposed framework empowers individuals by providing them control over their digital identities in line with SSI principles. It ensures the privacy and security of health records through the use of dynamic access control, thereby offering a comprehensive solution for healthcare systems.

The proposed framework addresses the security and privacy issues that are often found in centralized systems. It empowers users by granting them greater control over their digital identities, enabling them to determine and monitor precisely who has access to their health records. The framework effectively mitigates the risks of data leakage and preserves privacy through the use of Zero-Knowledge Proofs (ZKP) during the sharing and verification of credentials. It protects health records from unauthorized access by using a decentralized network. It eliminates the single point of failure issue that is common in centralized systems and provides a greater level of availability. Hyperledger Aries maintains an immutable audit trail of all activities, contributing to increased transparency and accountability. Hyperledger Indy utilizes a unique consensus algorithm known as *Plenum*, which provides a Byzantine Fault Tolerant (BFT) consensus mechanism. This mechanism ensures the reliability and consistency of the network. Indy's Plenum is a variant of *Redundant Byzantine Fault Tolerance* (RBFT) [3] and differs in the consensus round (3 phase commit) [1].

2.1   Components

Figure 1 provides an overview of the proposed framework and its components. In this figure, VC denotes Verifiable Credentials, VP is Verifiable Presentation, and VPR is Verifiable Presentation Request. The proposed framework includes the following components:

- **User:** A user is an entity that seeks to access medical data. Each user is uniquely identified by a Decentralized Identifiers (DID) and possesses their own SSI Agent Wallet, which stores a set of VCs issued by issuers, along with a public/private key pair associated with that DID. Examples include patients, doctors, or healthcare personnel.
- **Issuer/Trust Anchors (TAs):** The issuer or TA can be an individual or an organization (such as a government entity, insurance company, hospital, clinic, etc.) that is recognized and trusted by Hyperledger Indy. The issuer is responsible for issuing identities in the form of verifiable credentials to the holder and overseeing the revocation of identities when necessary. They are permitted to make entries in the ledger.

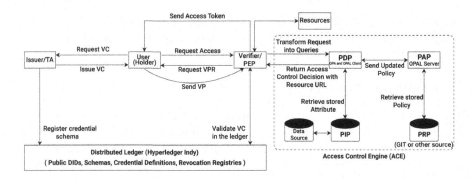

Fig. 1. The proposed framework with OPA

- **Verifier:** The verifier is the one who receives a request for access to the medical data from the user and verifies the user in the ledger. Following verification, verifiers initiate the access control request.
- **Indy Blockchain:** This is a permissioned public Hyperledger where anyone can read from the ledger, but only authorized principals can write on it. Built upon the Sovrin Foundation, its goal is to provide a blockchain-driven self-sovereign identity solution. It stores public DIDs, Schemas, Credential Definitions, Revocation registries, and their corresponding verification keys.
- **Access Control Engine (ACE):** The access control engine is a decentralized application or system that manages and enforces access control policies. It ensures that only authorized users or entities are granted the appropriate level of access while denying unauthorized access. By utilizing ABAC, it assesses verifiable credentials and translates them into actionable attributes, enabling precise authorization decisions.
- **Resources:** Resources, which are repositories for storing users' medical records, are located within the healthcare provider domains and are external to the ACE.

There are also some other components in Fig. 1, some of them are introduced due to the OPA integration:

- **Policy Enforcement Point (PEP):** This component in OPA serves as the system's gatekeeper. It redirects the decision to PDP. Subsequently, once the PDP component has rendered a decision, the PEP either grants or denies access to the requested resources.
- **Policy Decision Point (PDP):** The PDP plays a pivotal role in reaching the final decision, drawing upon the information it receives from both the PIP and PAP. In this capacity, the OPA and OPAL client function as the core PDP components in OPA.
- **Policy Administration Point (PAP):** In OPA, the OPAL (Open Policy Administration Layer) server operates as PAP. It retrieves stored policy from PRP.

- **Policy Retrieval Point (PRP):** In the context of OPA, the PRP serves as a repository for policies, which can be Git or other alternative sources.
- **Policy Information Point (PIP):** The OPAL client retrieves the latest attributes from the PIP, which, in turn, is linked to data sources for accessing the user's stored attributes.
- **Data Source:** This is an integral part of OPA, and is closely linked to PIPs. It serves as a secure repository for storing user attributes, which are retrieved by PIPs. These user attributes are stored as code within a Git repository, functioning as the data source in the OPA system.

2.2 Architecture

The proposed framework leverages Hyperledger Indy to establish SSI principles. Hyperledger Indy, through its Indy Node, forms the foundation for decentralized identity management. Within our framework, the User can be a patient, doctor, or healthcare personnel who wants to access medical data. All the actors such as the Issuer, User, and Verifier communicate with the Indy blockchain through their Hyperledger Aries agents. To receive VCs or access medical data, users must establish connections with both the Issuer and the Verifier. Users can store the issued VCs in their agent wallet. These stored VCs serve as a method for users to confirm their identity when seeking access to medical data. Figure 1 illustrates the architecture of the proposed framework.

The proposed framework deploys a dynamic ABAC policy, ensuring that access decisions are based on fine-grained attributes and policies. A strategic decision was made to opt for OPA as the ACE, as opposed to XACML (Extensible Access Control Markup Language). OPA offers a more straightforward and developer-friendly policy language called *Rego*, which allows for easier policy creation and management. In contrast, XACML uses XML-based policies, which can be complex and challenging to write and maintain, often requiring specialized expertise. Furthermore, OPA excels in scalability, efficiently managing numerous policies and access requests. In contrast, XACML may face performance issues when handling a high volume of access requests due to scalability limitations. Lastly, OPA's modern architecture seamlessly fits microservices, cloud-native, and containerized environments, whereas XACML's legacy design can complicate deployment in contemporary infrastructures.

The Verifier in the proposed framework has a dual function. Primarily, it acts as a Hyperledger Aries agent, facilitating seamless connectivity with the Indy node. In this capacity, it is responsible for verifying the identities of users and maintaining the integrity of the SSI ecosystem. Additionally, it also functions as a PEP component within an OPA-based system. This role allows it to enforce access control policies and ensure that authorization requests align with established policies. OPA incorporates both OPA and the OPAL client as PDPs that can be embedded in the verifier or be an external component. The centralized PDP is utilized in the proposed framework to increase throughput and lower latency compared with the decentralized PDP settings taken in [18] (and later in [22]).

2.3 Workflow

The workflow in the proposed framework comprises two distinct yet interrelated parts. The first part revolves around SSI, emphasizing user-centric control and ownership of digital identities. The second part of the workflow focuses on dynamic access control, where access to resources and services is governed by finely tuned attributes-based access control. Both of these workflow components work together to provide a comprehensive framework that incorporates the concepts of self-sovereign identity and dynamic access management.

2.3.1 SSI Workflow

In the SSI workflow, the seamless communication and interaction between key actors - including Issuer/Trust Anchors (TAs), Users, Verifiers, and the Hyperledger Indy framework - are facilitated by the Hyperledger Aries agents. These agents fill the gap between the actor's digital wallet and the Indy framework as essential middleware components. Hyperledger Aries offers a standardized communication protocol known as DIDComm for secure and private exchanges between participants. Below, we outline the steps involved in the SSI workflow as illustrated in Fig. 2:

1. The Issuer generates Schema and Credential Definition, and registers it in the ledger.
2. To create a secure communication between the issuer and user (e.g., patient, doctor, healthcare personnel), a pairwise DID has been generated and stored in their SSI agent wallet.
3. The Issuer then sends a credential offer to the user using the DIDComm protocol.
4. The User receives a notification to either approve or decline the offer. When the patient accepts, they initiate the process by sending a credential request to the Issuer.
5. The Issuer issues a VC and sends the issued VC to the User. This VC contains metadata, claims, and proofs using DIDComm.
6. The User then stores the VC in their wallet.
7. Prior to initiating a request for access to resources, such as medical data or patient health reports, a secure connection is established between the User and the Verifier.
8. User requests access to a set of resources.
9. The Verifier creates a VPR and sends it to the User.
10. After receiving the VPR from the Verifier, the User proceeds to generate a VP.
11. The user transmits the VP, which includes the essential attributes required for resource access, to the Verifier.
12. The Verifier initially operates as a Hyperledger Aries agent and verifies the proof in the Indy ledger.
13. The Indy ledger confirms the verification and a connection is established from the Indy ledger back to the Verifier, marking the successful verification loop.

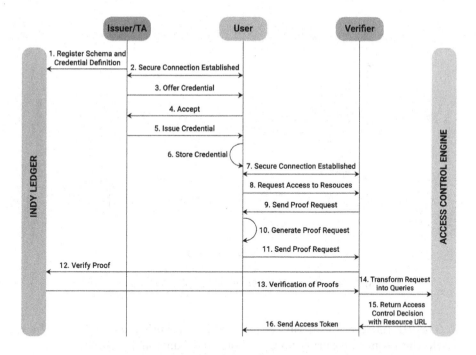

Fig. 2. SSI Implementation in the proposed framework

14. Subsequently, the Verifier assumes the role of a PEP and redirects access requests to the ACE for additional authorization.
15. Upon making an access control decision, the ACE communicates the result back to the Verifier, providing the final access control decision with the resource URL.
16. Following this, the Verifier sends an access token to the users.

2.3.2   Access Control Workflow

In the proposed framework, PDP, PAP, and PIP components within OPA collectively form a centralized part that is situated on the verifier side. The access control workflow in the proposed framework is depicted in Fig. 3, and its sequential steps can be followed as described below:

1. The Verifier, which operates as a PEP, takes the User's request and translates it into actionable attributes extracted from the VC. Subsequently, these attributes are sent to the OPA and the OPAL Client. OPAL collaborates with OPA and ensures the continuous real-time maintenance of the authorization layer.
2. The PDP then sends a request to PIP to fetch User attributes for the resources.

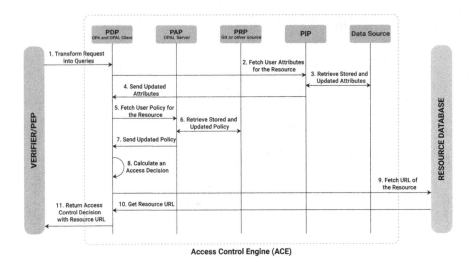

Fig. 3. Access Control Workflow in the proposed framework

3. The PIP retrieves the attributes required for the authorization decision from the data source, ensuring they are both up-to-date and accurate.
4. The PIP sends the updated attribute to the PDP.
5. The PDP proceeds to transmit a request to the OPAL server, which serves as a PAP, to retrieve the relevant policy pertaining to the requested resources.
6. In response, PAP retrieves the policy, which is both stored and updated, from the Git repository functioning as a PRP.
7. The PAP then sends PDP to the updated policy.
8. The PDP computes the access control decision by utilizing the up-to-date attributes and policy information.
9. In the event of access being granted, the PDP proceeds to retrieve the URL of the resource from the medical center's resource database. Conversely, if access is denied, the PDP promptly halts the authorization process.
10. If the access is granted PDP gets the URL link of the resources.
11. Following this, the PDP communicates the access decision, along with the resource's URL, back to the PEP, which subsequently returns the decision to the user.

3 Related Work

Blockchain-based access control has garnered significant attention in the research community, with extensive research conducted in recent years. Guo et al. [10] integrated blockchain and edge computing to manage access control for EHRs. The blockchain component is tasked with managing identity and access control, while the off-chain edge nodes store the EHR data and enforce ABAC policies. This hybrid architecture is designed to improve the scalability and efficiency of the system while maintaining data security and privacy. However, it may not have been tested in a real-world healthcare environment with a large-scale EHR system.

Abdelgalil et al. [2] proposed a blockchain framework that combines different technologies such as IPFS, Hyperledger Indy, and Hyperledger Fabric to address challenges associated with EHR sharing including data privacy, security, and interoperability. The proposed architecture may require significant investment in infrastructure and technology, which may be a barrier to adoption in some settings.

Saidi et al. [19] proposed DSMAC, a system for privacy-aware decentralized self-management of data access control based on blockchain for health data. DSMAC combines the RBAC approach, which manages access control to resources based on predefined roles, with the ABAC approach, which enables fine-grained access control in emergency situations. The architecture describes the evaluation of DSMAC using Hyperledger Indy. It considers SSI to improve the user identity model and uses several privacy-preserving techniques, such as encryption, ZKP, and anonymity, to achieve patient privacy and data confidentiality. The lack of implementation and real-world evaluation of the proposed DSMAC system restricts its practicality and effectiveness.

Haddad et al. [11] proposed a patient-centered blockchain-based EHR management system for efficient and secure management of medical data by patients across multiple stakeholders. The system uses the Ethereum blockchain and IPFS for the decentralized storage of EHRs, ensuring the immutability of records. However, the successful implementation and widespread adoption of the proposed scheme may encounter substantial obstacles, including scalability concerns, the need for standardization, and compliance with regulatory requirements.

Thwin and Vasupongayya [23] proposed a blockchain-based access control model for preserving privacy in personal health record (PHR) systems. The proposed model provides patients with control over their PHR data, allowing them to grant or revoke access to authorized users. The use of blockchain technology in the model enhances privacy, security, and transparency in PHR systems, offering potential benefits for healthcare data management. However, there is a need for additional research to address several outstanding challenges, including the facilitation of cross-border sharing of health data, as these issues could potentially impede the full realization of the benefits of blockchain-based data sharing in healthcare.

Chen et al. [7] introduced a blockchain-based medical data sharing mechanism that integrates ABAC and privacy protection. This scheme employs Hyperledger Fabric to enable data users to search for encrypted medical data records. They implemented K-anonymity and searchable encryption to ensure that medical data is shared without compromising privacy. However, the effectiveness and performance of their proposed scheme in a real-world scenario have not yet been evaluated.

Azbeg et al. [4] proposed a blockchain-based system for access control and privacy preservation in disease management with emphasize on security, scalability, and processing time. To address scalability issues in the blockchain-based system, they employed IPFS for storing a large volume of data. An Ethereum blockchain based on proof of authority (PoA) is utilized for faster data storage. However, one potential limitation could be its lack of a detailed analysis or validation of the proposed predictive model and decision-making processes.

Sun et al. [21] proposed a distributed electronic medical records (EMR) searchable scheme that uses blockchain and smart contract technology to achieve secure data sharing while preserving privacy. The integrity and authenticity of EMR are ensured through hash calculation and storage on the blockchain. Encrypted EMR data is stored in a distributed IPFS, which reduces the stress on data storage and high-frequency access to the blockchain. Attribute-based encryption is used to ensure that only users who meet the access policy can decrypt the encrypted EMR. However, their proposed scheme might have a limited focus on improving efficiency through edge-based solutions.

Gan et al. [9] proposed a blockchain-based access control scheme with an incentive mechanism for eHealth systems, in which patients act as supervisors. The scheme aims to ensure secure access to EHRs while incentivizing patients to supervise the access process. Patients are involved in the access decision-making process through a consensus mechanism, where their votes are recorded on the blockchain. Access requests are verified and recorded on the blockchain, and patients are rewarded with tokens for participating in the access control process. However, their proposed scheme exhibits limitations in terms of user authentication, availability, and anonymity.

Meier et al. [14] proposed a framework that combines blockchain technology with domain-specific design knowledge to ensure secure and privacy-preserving access control to PHRs. They emphasized the importance of incorporating domain-specific design knowledge, such as healthcare regulations and policies, into the design of blockchain-based access control systems. However, the practicality and feasibility of cooperation between various stakeholder groups on a blockchain-secured system are limited.

Torongo and Toorani [25] proposed BDIMHS, a decentralized identity management system for healthcare systems based on a permissioned blockchain with Hyperledger Indy and Hyperledger Aries. Their proposed solution enhances data security, privacy, immutability, interoperability, and patient autonomy by employing selective disclosure, ZKPs, DIDs, and VCs. However, they did not delve into the access control aspect.

Belchior et al. [6] proposed an SSI-Based Access Control (SSIBAC) model that provides a promising solution for cross-organization identity management. This model combines decentralized authentication with centralized authorization, eliminating the need to store sensitive user data. The central concept of SSIBAC is to link VCs with access control policies, which are interpreted by an underlying access control model to establish context-based privileges. However, it has a significant limitation: verifiers serve as the central ACE, creating a single point of failure. This single point of failure can pose a critical risk to the system's trust and reliability, especially in a decentralized and trustless blockchain-based environment.

Rouhani et al. [18] proposed a distributed ABAC system based on Hyperledger Fabric and smart contracts. They proposed a distributed setting for PDP based on XACML. Building upon this, Tadjik et al. [22] further refined Rouhani et al.'s concept [18], proposing the SSIDD scheme which utilizes Hyperledger Indy, Hyperledger Fabric, IPFS, and XACML. Our proposed solution, distinguishes itself from the aforementioned works in several key aspects. Firstly, it eliminates the need for smart contracts and Hyperledger Fabric, which significantly enhances performance due to decreased complexity and workload. Secondly, its architecture is based on OPA rather than XACML as mentioned in Sect. 2.2.

4   Conclusion

In this paper, we introduced a blockchain-based access control framework designed to enhance the security and privacy of EHRs. It addresses the critical challenges of securing and managing medical data access while providing individuals with SSI and enhancing their privacy. As part of our future work, we will delve deeper into the functionalities of the components within the proposed framework, providing a formal and comprehensive description. We plan to bring the proposed framework to life by implementing a prototype using Hyperledger Indy and Aries, and subsequently testing its efficacy in a realistic environment. Furthermore, our future work encompasses an exhaustive performance and security analysis. This will not only allow us to refine and fortify the proposed framework but also substantiate the security claims we have made.

Acknowledgement. This work is partially supported by the Norwegian Research Council under project number 331903.

References

1. Indy Plenum's documentation. https://hyperledger-indy.readthedocs.io/projects/plenum/en/latest/main.html. Accessed 15 Oct 2023
2. Abdelgalil, L., Mejri, M.: HealthBlock: a framework for a collaborative sharing of electronic health records based on blockchain. Future Internet **15**(3), 87 (2023)
3. Aublin, P., Mokhtar, S.B., Quéma, V.: RBFT: redundant byzantine fault tolerance. In: IEEE 33rd International Conference on Distributed Computing Systems, ICDCS 2013, Philadelphia, Pennsylvania, USA, 8–11 July 2013, pp. 297–306. IEEE Computer Society (2013). https://doi.org/10.1109/ICDCS.2013.53
4. Azbeg, K., Ouchetto, O., Jai Andaloussi, S.: Access control and privacy-preserving blockchain-based system for diseases management. IEEE Trans. Comput. Soc. Syst. **10**(4), 1515–1527 (2023). https://doi.org/10.1109/TCSS.2022.3186945
5. Bauer, D.P.: InterPlanetary File System, pp. 83–96. Apress, Berkeley, (2022). https://doi.org/10.1007/978-3-4842-8045-4_7

6. Belchior, R., Putz, B., Pernul, G., Correia, M., Vasconcelos, A., Guerreiro, S.: SSIBAC: self-sovereign identity based access control. In: Wang, G., Ko, R.K.L., Bhuiyan, M.Z.A., Pan, Y. (eds.) 19th IEEE International Conference on Trust, Security and Privacy in Computing and Communications, TrustCom 2020, Guangzhou, China, 29 December 2020–1 January 2021, pp. 1935–1943. IEEE (2020). https://doi.org/10.1109/TrustCom50675.2020.00264

7. Chen, Y., Meng, L., Zhou, H., Xue, G.: A blockchain-based medical data sharing mechanism with attribute-based access control and privacy protection. Wirel. Commun. Mob. Comput. **2021**, 1–12 (2021)

8. Daraghmi, E.Y., Daraghmi, Y., Yuan, S.: Medchain: a design of blockchain-based system for medical records access and permissions management. IEEE Access **7**, 164595–164613 (2019). https://doi.org/10.1109/ACCESS.2019.2952942

9. Gan, C., Saini, A., Zhu, Q., Xiang, Y., Zhang, Z.: Blockchain-based access control scheme with incentive mechanism for ehealth systems: patient as supervisor. Multim. Tools Appl. **80**(20), 30605–30621 (2021). https://doi.org/10.1007/s11042-020-09322-6

10. Guo, H., Li, W., Nejad, M.M., Shen, C.: Access control for electronic health records with hybrid blockchain-edge architecture. In: IEEE International Conference on Blockchain, Blockchain 2019, Atlanta, GA, USA, 14–17 July 2019, pp. 44–51. IEEE (2019). https://doi.org/10.1109/Blockchain.2019.00015

11. Haddad, A., Habaebi, M.H., Suliman, F.E.M., Elsheikh, E.A.A., Islam, M.R., Zabidi, S.A.: Generic patient-centered blockchain-based EHR management system. Appl. Sci. **13**(3) (2023). https://doi.org/10.3390/app13031761

12. Han, Y., Zhang, Y., Vermund, S.H.: Blockchain technology for electronic health records. Int. J. Environ. Res. Public Health **19**(23) (2022). https://doi.org/10.3390/ijerph192315577. https://www.mdpi.com/1660-4601/19/23/15577

13. Houtan, B., Hafid, A.S., Makrakis, D.: A survey on blockchain-based self-sovereign patient identity in healthcare. IEEE Access **8**, 90478–90494 (2020). https://doi.org/10.1109/ACCESS.2020.2994090

14. Meier, P., Beinke, J.H., Fitte, C., Brinke, J.S., Teuteberg, F.: Generating design knowledge for blockchain-based access control to personal health records. Inf. Syst. E Bus. Manag. **19**(1), 13–41 (2021). https://doi.org/10.1007/s10257-020-00476-2

15. Olsson, C., Toorani, M.: A permissioned blockchain-based system for collaborative drug discovery. In: Mori, P., Lenzini, G., Furnell, S. (eds.) Proceedings of the 7th International Conference on Information Systems Security and Privacy, ICISSP 2021, Online Streaming, 11–13 February 2021, pp. 121–132. SCITEPRESS (2021). https://doi.org/10.5220/0010236901210132

16. Preukschat, A., Reed, D.: Self-sovereign Identity. Manning Publications, New York (2021)

17. Quantin, C., Coatrieux, G., Fassa, M., Breton, V., Jaquet-Chiffelle, D.: Centralised versus decentralised management of patients' medical records. In: Adlassnig, K., Blobel, B., Mantas, J., Masic, I. (eds.) Medical Informatics in a United and Healthy Europe - Proceedings of MIE 2009, The XXIInd International Congress of the European Federation for Medical Informatics, Sarajevo, Bosnia and Herzegovina, 30 August–2 September 2009. Studies in Health Technology and Informatics, vol. 150, pp. 700–704. IOS Press (2009). https://doi.org/10.3233/978-1-60750-044-5-700

18. Rouhani, S., Belchior, R., Cruz, R.S., Deters, R.: Distributed attribute-based access control system using permissioned blockchain. World Wide Web **24**(5), 1617–1644 (2021). https://doi.org/10.1007/s11280-021-00874-7

19. Saidi, H., Labraoui, N., Ari, A.A.A., Maglaras, L.A., Emati, J.H.M.: DSMAC: privacy-aware decentralized self-management of data access control based on blockchain for health data. IEEE Access **10**, 101011–101028 (2022). https://doi.org/10.1109/ACCESS.2022.3207803

20. Shuaib, K., Abdella, J., Sallabi, F., Serhani, M.A.: Secure decentralized electronic health records sharing system based on blockchains. J. King Saud Univ. Comput. Inf. Sci. **34**(8, Part A), 5045–5058 (2022). https://doi.org/10.1016/j.jksuci.2021.05.002. https://www.sciencedirect.com/science/article/pii/S1319157821001051

21. Sun, J., Ren, L., Wang, S., Yao, X.: A blockchain-based framework for electronic medical records sharing with fine-grained access control. PLoS ONE **15**(10), e0239946 (2020). https://doi.org/10.1371/journal.pone.0239946

22. Tadjik, H., Geng, J., Jaatun, M.G., Rong, C.: Blockchain empowered and self-sovereign access control system. In: 2022 IEEE International Conference on Cloud Computing Technology and Science (CloudCom), pp. 74–82. IEEE (2022)

23. Thwin, T.T., Vasupongayya, S.: Blockchain-based access control model to preserve privacy for personal health record systems. Secur. Commun. Networks **2019**, 8315614:1–8315614:15 (2019). https://doi.org/10.1155/2019/8315614

24. Toorani, M., Gehrmann, C.: A decentralized dynamic PKI based on blockchain. In: Hung, C., Hong, J., Bechini, A., Song, E. (eds.) SAC 2021: The 36th ACM/SIGAPP Symposium on Applied Computing, Virtual Event, Republic of Korea, 22–26 March 2021, pp. 1646–1655. ACM (2021). https://doi.org/10.1145/3412841.3442038

25. Torongo, A.A., Toorani, M.: Blockchain-based decentralized identity management for healthcare systems. CoRR abs/2307.16239 (2023). https://doi.org/10.48550/arXiv.2307.16239

26. Wu, X., Han, Y., Zhang, M., Zhu, S.: Secure personal health records sharing based on blockchain and IPFS. In: Han, W., Zhu, L., Yan, F. (eds.) CTCIS 2019. CCIS, vol. 1149, pp. 340–354. Springer, Singapore (2020). https://doi.org/10.1007/978-981-15-3418-8_22

Privacy Risks, and Resilience in Healthcare Systems

Threat Modeling Towards Resilience in Smart ICUs

Christian Baumhör[1], Thomas Henning[1], and Matteo Große-Kampmann[1,2(✉)] 📷

[1] AWARE7 GmbH, Gelsenkirchen, Germany
{christian,thomas}@aware7.de
[2] Rhine-Waal University of Applied Sciences, Kamp-Lintfort, Germany
matteo.grosse-kampmann@hochschule-rhein-waal.de
https://aware7.com

Abstract. Healthcare digitization has significantly enhanced patient care and alleviated the workload of hospital staff. This trend towards automation has also optimized the intensive care units (ICUs) of hospitals, leading to the emergence of smart ICUs equipped with modern wireless communication networks like 5G. However, this increased digitization presents new attack vectors and opportunities, especially regarding cybersecurity attacks. These attacks could compromise the resilience of smart ICU networks. Given the critical role of ICUs in healthcare, it is imperative to analyze and categorize digital threats in terms of the risks they pose to patients. This paper explores cybersecurity threats for smart ICU networks and offers a risk assessment of the potential worst-case impacts these threats could have on the network.

1 Introduction

Digital failures in healthcare settings, especially in an Intensive Care Unit (ICU), can have severe repercussions, potentially jeopardizing the treatment of critical clinical cases. With the escalating integration of digital technologies into ICUs, these units transform into 'smart ICUs', enabling the automatic patient treatment, remote expert consultation, and even robot-assisted surgeries directly in the ICU (Anderson et al. 2018). To achieve the desired flexibility and mobility of devices, these intelligent ICUs increasingly rely on modern mobile communication networks, particularly 5G (Peralta-Ochoa et al. 2023).

Understanding its cybersecurity threats becomes a paramount issue as the ICU environment becomes digitized. We define the stability of the ICU environment in terms of resilience, a construct we further delineate using the resilience categories of *Respond, Learn, Anticipate,* and *Monitor* (Salluh et al. 2022; Hollnagel 2015; Eliash et al. 2020). This paper seeks to bridge the gap between cybersecurity threats and smart ICU resilience.

This research was funded by the Federal Ministry of Research and Education Healthnet (FKZ: 16KISR001K) and the Federal Office for Information Security Pentest-5GSec (FKZ: 01MO23025A).

H. Abie et al. (Eds.): SUNRISE 2023, CCIS 1884, pp. 37–50, 2024.
https://doi.org/10.1007/978-3-031-55829-0_3

We provide a digital threat analysis within the context of smart ICUs based partly on mobile communication (Mayol et al. 2016). We employ the CIA (confidentiality, integrity, and availability) framework to classify the digital threats associated with distinct network components. Additionally, we conduct a risk analysis of worst-case scenarios within the smart ICU network, thus contributing to the design principles and metrics for cyber-resilient systems.

In summary, our paper offers the following primary contributions to the field:

– A digital threat model for smart ICU networks, partly based on mobile communication, within the CIA framework.
– A risk analysis of the most severe threats within the smart ICU network, contributing to developing cyber-resilient systems.

2 Background

This section presents the background information for understanding the threat modeling introduced in Sect. 5.

2.1 Digitization and Resilience of Healthcare

The advent of the Internet of Things (IoT) has revolutionized healthcare by enabling the integration of a wide range of devices into networked systems, paving the way for mobile health systems and smart hospital environments (Kotz et al. 2016; Martnez-Prez et al. 2014; Mayol et al. 2016). According to the European Union Agency for Cybersecurity (ENISA), an intelligent hospital capitalizes on interconnected ICT assets, particularly IoT-based, to optimize and automate processes, enhance patient care, and introduce new capabilities (Mayol et al. 2016). This sentiment is echoed by Bullen et al., who posit that smart hospitals, powered by intelligent technologies and facilities, foster a superior environment for patients (Bullen et al. 2017).

Within this context, the Intensive Care Unit (ICU) is a critical component. The unique requirements and specialized treatment methods necessitate specific equipment and IoT devices, making a smart ICU a distinct entity within the smart hospital. Anderson et al. have constructed a prototype of such a smart ICU network (Anderson et al. 2018).

Resilience is critical to healthcare, especially in specialized facilities like the ICU (Mayol et al. 2016). In the face of a global pandemic such as COVID-19, ICU resilience is crucial. Salluh et al. propose an ICU resilience framework based on Hollnagel's resilience assessment grid, delineating several ICU resilience factors that ensure robust operation even in a pandemic scenario (Salluh et al. 2022; Hollnagel 2015).

2.2 5G Networks in Healthcare

Mobile communication will play an integral part in a digital hospital environment. The need for reliability and real-time data processing, particularly in ICUs, underscores the importance of the mobile communication technology chosen.

5G networks, with their superior speed, lower latency, and larger bandwidth compared to 4G, are ideal for building internal or campus networks, including hospital and ICU networks (Peralta-Ochoa et al. 2023). The real-time, high-volume data transmission capability of 5G makes it invaluable in a healthcare setting. It is especially beneficial in cases of robotic remote surgeries, enhancing the precision and responsiveness of the procedure (Mao et al. 2023).

3   Related Work

Prior research has introduced threat modeling in the context of healthcare systems. These papers discussed threats in a hospital environment (Mayol et al. 2016), for mobile health systems (Cagnazzo et al. 2018), and even for ICU devices (Eliash et al. 2020). However, to our knowledge, prior work has yet to analyze the intersection of cybersecurity resilience and ICU resilience, mainly focusing on modern mobile communication networks in a smart ICU context. This is becoming an important aspect due to both improved computer performance (Winkelhake 2017), as well as on the basis of the exponentially growing amount of data in the ternet (Tenzer 2023). Furthermore, more complex applications of artificial intelligence in healthcare have established themselves in the healthcare sector. However, these are often isolated solutions that are not always used in the context of cross-border networking (Plugmann 2022). This is where 5G communication comes in and offers many opportunities in the health offers many opportunities in the healthcare sector by accelerating data transmission and improving the networking of medical devices and applications.

3.1   History of Mobile Communication

The first generation (1G) of mobile networks should be mentioned as precursors to the 5th generation of mobile communications. They were in operation from 1958 until 2000. This made analog voice transmission to mobile devices possible, which did not have a uniform standard (Leidinger et al. 2020).

Digital transmission was introduced in 1992 with the introduction of the second generation (2G) mobile network (see Fig. 2). This enabled a significant improvement in voice quality to be achieved. In addition, for the first time in Europe, a Global System for Mobile Communications (GSM) has been achieved to create a European standard. Text messages could now be transmitted between two devices using the Short Message Service (SMS). Photos can also be sent through General Packet Radio Service (GPRS) and Enhanced Data Rates for GSM Evolution (EDGE) or simple websites can be visited (Leidinger et al. 2020).

Due to the significantly higher data rates, the third generation of mobile communications (3G) and the Universal Mobile Telecommunications Standard (UMTS) developed for it made nationwide, mobile use of the Internet possible. The two UMTS extensions, Highspeed Packet Access (HSPA) and HSPA+, also made it possible to achieve significantly higher transmission rates. The fourth generation of mobile networks (4G) went into operation for the first time in

2010 at the same time as the Long Term Evolution (LTE) standard. The main advantage, in addition to a faster data rate, was lower latency between the transmitter and receiver. Another characteristic feature was the better reception and voice quality, as well as low energy consumption and a higher level of security. A second development stage for LTE-Advanced was again characterized by higher data rates and lower latency (Leidinger et al. 2020).

Since 2018, there has been a standard for the 5G Radio Access Network (RAN) through the 3rd Generation Partnership Projects (3GPP) TS 38.4011, which is similar to the LTE standard in some points. The 5G technology has been standardized much more flexibly in order to ensure greater compatibility (Leidinger et al. 2020). In general, due to market pressure, the 5G system was pushed to be introduced as quickly as possible. This was realized by the 5G Non-Standalone Architecture (NSA) networks. For this purpose, the existing LTE radio and core networks are used as an environment for the 5G radio cells. Prospectively, the entire 4G network is to be replaced by 5G components. This would make usage scenarios such as narrow-band machine type communication (MTC), lower latency and different quality-of-service mechanisms possible. As soon as networks are deployed that only use a 5G core network, it is also easier to realize new functionalities such as lower latency and very high transmission security (Lin 2018; Tunder 2020).

3.2   Smart Intensive Care Unit

Our threat modeling builds upon the smart ICU network approach proposed by Anderson et al. (2018). The ICU network is conceptualized as an internal envelope encapsulating all hardware used for patient care. This envelope communicates with the hospital network (the outer envelope) via hardware and software middleware. This paper focuses on the internal envelope and the threats concerning the resilience of the local ICU network.

The components of the smart ICU network are categorized. The first category, *Alarm Systems*, aims to mitigate noise overload from various ICU systems and relay alarms to relevant stakeholders, such as the nearest nurses. The *Automatic Medication Dosing* category houses components that automate patient-specific medication. *Virtual Device Communities* groups similar devices, like monitors or cameras, to streamline software upgrades and facilitate shared data storage and remote viewing. *Real-Time Locating Systems* track devices and personnel, while *Environmental Monitoring* involves monitoring room temperature, oxygen saturation, and using cameras for team communication. The *Data Integration, Smart Displays, and Decision Support* category uses collected data to detect patient vital abnormalities and inform potential treatment steps. Several components of the smart ICU utilize mobile communication. For example, ventilation machines and infusion pumps are wirelessly connected to other gadgets in the *Alarm Systems* and *Automatic Medication Dosing* categories. The high bandwidth of a 5G ICU network makes it suitable for this task, connecting middleware and patient room components and supporting telemedicine (Peralta- Ochoa et al. 2023).

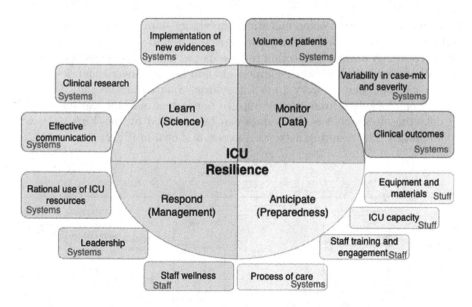

Fig. 1. ICU Resilience Framework

Thus, a resilient 5G network is crucial for ensuring cybersecurity resilience in an ICU context, with Wi-Fi as a fallback option.

3.3   Intensive Care Unit Resilience

When discussing ICU Resilience, we refer to the framework provided by Salluh et al. (2022), based on Hollnagel's Resilience Assessment Grid (Hollnagel 2015). This grid models system resilience based on the four pillars: *Respond, Learn, Anticipate,* and *Monitor.* The resulting ICU resilience factors align with the 4S (staff, stuff, space, systems) used to define health system resilience generally (Alomani et al. 2022). For our threat modeling, we discard the factor *Improved ICU outcomes*, as it is implied by the other three factors related to Hollnagel's category *Respond* (Salluh et al. 2022). Figure 1 illustrates the ICU resilience framework.

ENISA has already modeled threats for smart hospitals (Mayol et al. 2016), but this model needs to sufficiently account for modern hospital equipment interconnected via mobile communication networks. We consider ENISA's work and map it to the smart ICU network's internal envelope and middleware (Anderson et al. 2018).

4   Method

We adopt the smart ICU network concept (Anderson et al. 2018) to construct our network. Specifically, we focus on the internal ICU network, which utilizes middleware for external communication, servers for data processing, and a virtual device controller, which groups similar devices and servers for administrative purposes. A dashed connection represents the use of a wireless 5G connection. We categorize all network components and further break them down into specific gadgets. The category *Data Integration, Smart Displays, and Decision Support* employs data from other groups to populate a machine learning model for detecting abnormalities. This data can be prepared by the *Virtual Device Communities*. The resulting network diagram is shown in Fig. 2.

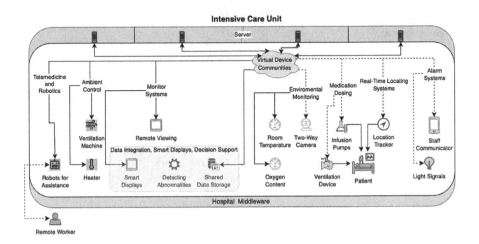

Fig. 2. Smart ICU Network Diagram

We first identify if a network component category impacts an ICU resilience factor to establish a relationship between the smart ICU network and ICU resilience factors. We then apply the CIA framework to model threats of smart ICU networks. Each cybersecurity threat is mapped to at least one smart ICU network category, indicating its impact on the *confidentiality, integrity,* or *availability* of that specific component category. The outcome is a model of threats to ICU resilience from the perspective of cybersecurity resilience.

To assess the risk of each threat, we utilize the risk assessment framework provided by ENISA (2017), Mayol et al. (2016). This process involves a quantitative evaluation that combines the likelihood of a threat occurring and its potential impact on data processing operations.

The first aspect of risk assessment involves estimating the probability of a threat eventuating. This is achieved by analyzing historical data, security incidents, threat intelligence, and other relevant sources. The probability can be assigned a low, medium, or high qualitative rating.

The second aspect is to assess the potential impact of the threat on data processing operations and overall system security. This involves considering the severity of consequences on the data's confidentiality, integrity, and availability (CIA). For example, a high-impact threat could result in significant data breaches, loss of critical information, or system downtime. In contrast, a low-impact threat might cause minor disruptions.

To quantify the risk associated with a particular threat, we combine the probability and impact values, often represented as risk values. The risk value aids in prioritizing threats that require immediate attention and those risks that can be addressed later. A high impact always results in a high risk value.

5   Results

To link cybersecurity resilience and ICU resilience, we provide two steps. First, we connect the categories of the smart ICU network to the ICU resilience factors. Afterwards, we map cybersecurity threats to the smart ICU network component categories. The overall result indicates a transitive connection from threats with respect to cybersecurity to ICU resilience. In addition, we provide the worst-case risk assessment for each threat.

5.1   Mapping Smart ICU Network Categories to ICU Resilience Factors

In the following we map the ICU resilience factors (Salluh et al. 2022) to the categories of network components in a smart ICU network (Anderson et al. 2018). Therefore, we tell whether a factor is impaired by compromise of a network component category. The first factors we address are the *Respond* (Management) factors. **Rational use of ICU resources** is affected by the categories *Alarm Systems*, *Automatic Medication Dosing* and *Telemedicine and Robotics*. Failure of these categories implies wrong usage of the resources medicine, with non-correct dosing, as well as staff, because alarms can be sent out to a wrong number of people, or remote workers are cut off the hospital network.

With factor **leadership** we need to take the network categories *Real-Time Locating Systems* and *Virtual Device Communities* into account. Both categories help deciders to overlook the staff and the current status of the ICU.

Staff wellness is affected by all systems, because any system that fails has to be compensated by the staff. Hence, the staff can be stressed, if any system does not work properly.

The next three factors we discuss are related to *Learn* (Science). **Implementation of new evidences** cannot be done properly, if the *Data Integration* support works incorrect. It is also problematic, if the remote work aspect from *Telemedicine and Robotics* is limited.

To offer **effective communication**, smart ICU networks use many systems for different kinds of communication. *Alarm Systems* are used for concrete scenarios to acquire help, *Real-Time Locating Systems* can be used to omit communication steps with respect to staff being around and *Environmental Monitoring* is used to offer intercoms for direct communication. Moreover, *Virtual Device Communities* merge communication devices to groups for administrative reasons. With *Telemedicine and Robotics* being the interface for communication partners outside the inner envelope, it is also an important category for effective communication.

For integration of own **clinical research**, any measurement system is important. This includes *Real-Time Locating Systems* and *Environmental Monitoring* for the external circumstances, *Virtual Device Communities* and *Data Integration, Smart Displays, and Decision Support* for data evaluation, as well as *Telemedicine and Robotics* for dialogue between experts.

Associated to *Anticipate* (Preparedness) are four factors. **Equipment and materials** is preserved by protection of *Medication Dosing, Virtual Device Communities* and *Telemedicine and Robotics*. All three categories are used to organize the ICU's equipment and consumables.

Three categories affect **staff training and engagement**. *Alarm Systems* tell the ICU staff where engagement is needed, whereas *Data Integration, Smart Displays, and Decision Support* tells them what engagement is needed. For remote training, the category *Telemedicine and Robotics* is used.

Regarding the factor **ICU capacity** with respect to preparedness, all ICU network categories are included, that can be used to higher the number of admitted patients, if needed. This includes *Alarm Systems*, to increase the staff temporarily, *Automatic Medication Dosing*, for a suitable medication, without further human interaction, but also *Decision Support* and *Telemedicine and Robotics* to use computer systems for assistance.

With the identical reasons, the same categories of network systems are used to provide an appropriate **process of care**.

The last part of Hollnagel's Resilience Assessment Grid stands for *Monitor* (Data). To overview **clinical outcomes**, *Automatic Medication Dosing* can be used for tracking the correct administering of medicine to patients. The categories *Data Integration, Smart Displays, and Decision Support* and *Telemedicine and Robotics* are also considered, because the data has to be collected and be made accessible outside the ICU.

To monitor **variability in case-mix and severity**, the same three categories *Automatic Medication Dosing, Data Integration, Smart Displays, and Decision Support* and *Telemedicine and Robotics* are involved, but also the *Alarm Systems* are useful to track the number of critical situations.

The last factor for ICU resilience is the **volume of patients**. The main category of systems that is used to monitor the volume is *Real-Time Locating Systems*. The categories *Environmental Monitoring* and *Virtual Device Communities* need to work as anticipated as well, since wrong outputs lead to an incorrect tracking of the volume of patients.

5.2   Mapping Cybersecurity Threats to Smart ICU Network Component Categories

Now that we know what categories of components in the smart ICU network affect which factors of a resilient ICU, we can take the cybersecurity threats into account. We will focus on concrete digital threats (Mayol et al. 2016) and decide, if the *confidentiality*, *integrity* or *availability* of a smart ICU network component category is affected.

The first cybersecurity threat is **session hijacking**. To hijack a session, an attacker must be able to obtain a security token that is used to authenticate within a communication. Hence, all devices that use sessions between servers and clients can be prone to session hijacking. Especially components that use the mobile communication network are in focus, as an attacker can interact with the 5G network without plugging a device into a port inside the ICU. The *Automatic Medication Dosing* systems have to use sessions with respect to each patient. Getting the session token enables to break the CONFIDENTIALITY, INTEGRITY and AVAILABILITY of the system, as an attacker is able to disclose, change and deny a patient's medication. The same applies for *Virtual Device Communities* and *Telemedicine and Robotics*, because an attacker can watch, change and delete data stored or communicated in both categories. The two categories *Real-Time Locating Systems* and *Data Integration, Smart Displays, and Decision Support* can also be session hijacked. In this case only the CONFIDENTIALITY of data is concerned, since a session enables to only read the stored data.

A large group of threats is the use of **malware**. It includes trojans, viruses, worms, ransomware and more. With ransomware and viruses, an attacker is able to deny access to any data in the network or even shutdown all systems. This implies that all systems are prone to malware in terms of AVAILABILITY. With the ability to run code on a system, an attacker can get information of stored or captured data of the systems and even change the data within the capturing process or in the storage. Hence, also CONFIDENTITALITY and INTEGRITY of all systems are affected by malware. With access to the 5G network, an attacker is able to interact with components within the smart ICU, after installing a backdoor, by using malware.

Well known threats are **denial of service attacks** and **power failures**. Both threats address the AVAILABILITY of a system. All systems run with electric power and all systems handle incoming connections. Particularly, the wireless 5G devices that handle incoming connections are prone to denial of service attacks, due to the fact that an overload of requests cannot be handled. Hence, the devices are unreachable for other ICU components. All systems are prone to the threats.

Another typical attack scenario is **social engineering**. There are two system categories that are prone to social engineering. By imitating a family member, someone could get insides of the *Automatic Medication Dosing* of a specific patient, which breaks the CONFIDENTIALITY of the system. By phishing attacks, someone could even get remote expert access in the *Telemedicine and Robotics* category. With this access, the attacker is able to obtain and change data, which breaks the CONFIDENTIALITY and INTEGRITY of the category.

Damaged hardware often leads to an AVAILABILITY problem of certain systems. This is a typical threat for all network categories. In case of *Automatic Medication Dosing* this threat can also yield to a patient changing the medication dosing on its own. Hence, even the INTEGRITY of the system is affected.

A common mistake is an **erroneous configuration** of the systems. *Alarm Systems* may not deliver the alarm to all necessary groups. The *Automatic Medication Dosing* does not consider all medications that have to be used for a patient. For *Virtual Device Communities, Data Integration, Smart Displays, and Decision Support* and *Telemedicine and Robotics* data can be made inaccessible by misconfiguration. Hence, these systems may have an AVAILABILITY problem by erroneous configuration. Like in case of damaged hardware, misconfiguration for *Automatic Medication Dosing* systems may enable patients to change the dosing on their own, which is an INTEGRITY incident. In case of *Virtual Device Communities* and *Telemedicine and Robotics* a wrong configuration can leak data to third parties, that access components in the mobile communication network, or even enable third parties to change the data. Therefore, both categories are additionally threatened in terms of CONFIDENTIALITY and INTEGRITY.

With *Telemedicine and Robotics* being the ICU network category that handles remote work through a 5G connection, CONFIDENTIALITY, INTEGRITY and AVAILABILITY are threatened by **non-compliance with security guidelines**. This includes correct storage of passwords that are used for remote logins, or correct locking of hardware in the public.

Missing authorization checks are problematic for all systems that show specific data, or even let people interact with the data. All systems process data of a specific kind and hence, all systems have a CONFIDENTIALITY matter, if there is no authorization check to interact with the system. The ease of interaction with a 5G network underlines the importance of authorization checks for all categories that make use of it. The categories *Automatic Medication Dosing, Virtual Device Communities* and *Telemedicine and Robotics*, that are connected to the mobile network, even allow the change of data within the system. Hence, there is an INTEGRITY issue.

All systems are prone to **data theft**, which affects the CONFIDENTIALITY of all smart ICU network component categories.

5.3   Transitive Relation Between Cybersecurity Threats and ICU Resilience Factors

With respect to the smart ICU network (Anderson et al. 2018) and the CIA framework, we receive a transitive cybersecurity resilience to ICU resilience relation, as shown in Table 1. The table shows a threat modeling of the smart hospital's cybersecurity threats (Mayol et al. 2016) to the four pillars of Hollnagel's resilience assessment grid in terms of ICU resilience (Salluh et al. 2022) (*Respond, Learn, Anticipate* and *Monitor*). If a threat, related to at least one of the pillar's factors, affects confidentiality (C), integrity (I) or availability (A), the according letter is added to the matching.

The cybersecurity threats **session hijacking, malware, erroneous configuration** and **non-compliance with security guidelines** impact CONFIDENTIALITY, INTEGRITY and AVAILABILITY of all four Hollnagel pillars.

AVAILABILITY is affected in all four pillars, for the threats **denial of service attacks** and **power failures**.

Table 1. Intersection Cybersecurity Resilience and ICU Resilience

Threat	Respond	Learn	Anticipate	Monitor
Session hijacking	CIA	CIA	CIA	CIA
Malware	CIA	CIA	CIA	CIA
Denial of service attack	A	A	A	A
Social engineering	CI	CI	CI	CI
Damaged hardware	IA	A	IA	IA
Erroneous configuration	CIA	CIA	CIA	CIA
No guideline compliance	CIA	CIA	CIA	CIA
Power failures	A	A	A	A
No authorization checks	CI	CI	CI	CI
Data theft	C	C	C	C

The threat of **data theft** leads to a possible CONFIDENTIALITY problem.

With **social engineering** and **missing authorization checks** all pillars have CONFIDENTIALITY and INTEGRITY risks.

Damaged hardware may lead to an AVAILABILITY issue in all Hollnagel pillars. It also can impact the INTEGRITY of the pillars *Respond, Anticipate* and *Monitor*.

Note that resilience of the mobile communication network is required to ensure resilience in all four Hollnagel pillars.

5.4   Risk Assessment

In the previous sections we discussed possible threats for the smart ICU environment and its relation to ICU resilience. In the following we want to discuss the impact and occurrence probability of the threats in the worst-case. We will then use the risk evaluation method of the ENISA (2017), to conclude a risk assessment. Table 2 shows the determined values for impact and occurrence probability, as well as the resulting risk value.

With ICUs operating on almost exclusively highly sensitive data and focus on rescuing human lives, we need to consider a customized risk assessment as long as ICU networks are concerned, than for common digital threats. Since this paper focuses on threats regarding the local ICU network and does not consider the rest of the hospital, we will label the impact of a threat's worst-case appearance as follows:

- **High:** The threat can endanger human lives or harm the patient.
- **Medium:** Highly sensitive personal data can be stolen, tampered or made inaccessible.
- **Low:** No patient is harmed and no highly sensitive data is involved.

Table 2. Risk Evaluation Table for Smart ICU Threats

Threat	Impact	Occurrence Prob.	Risk
Session hijacking	High	Medium	High
Malware	High	High	High
Denial of service attack	High	High	High
Social engineering	High	High	High
Damaged hardware	High	Low	High
Erroneous configuration	High	High	High
No guideline compliance	High	High	High
Power failures	High	High	High
No authorization checks	High	High	High
Data theft	Medium	Medium	Medium

This enables us to classify the risks for the specific context of an ICU network. Note that a risk assessment for a complete hospital environment would look different, as for example the loss of sensitive data would be ranked higher.

The impact of all discussed threats but **data theft** is ranked as high, since a triggering of the threat could at least harm a patient. With **session hijacking, malware, social engineering, erroneous configuration, non-compliance with security guidelines** and **missing authorization checks**, the integrity of a remote expert surgery is affected. Hence, a human life is endangered. With a **denial of service attack, power failure** and **damaged hardware**, the availability of the automatic medication dosing system is under risk. Through this, a patient can be seriously harmed. **Data theft** is ranked as medium, because in the worst-case sensitive data can be stolen.

To determine the occurrence probability for **session hijacking, malware** and **denial of service attacks**, we rely on the attack complexity calculated by Eliash et al. (2020). Therefore, we rank the probability as medium for session hijacking and high for malware and denial of service attacks. With **social engineering** being realizable without further technical knowledge, the occurrence probability is high. An opinion poll, performed by the ENISA (Mayol et al. 2016), ranked the likelihood of social engineering as high as the likelihood of denial of service attacks. The threats **erroneous configuration, non-compliance with security guidelines** and **missing authorization checks** are triggered by human errors. Studies (Mee and Brandenburg 2020) show, that human errors are the most common cause of security breaches, which makes the occurrence probability also high. The case of **damaged hardware** has a low probability, as such errors on the part of the manufacturer are less frequently. The probability of a **power failure** is classified as high. Evidence gives a statistic that shows that in 2018 were about 7 power outages in firms worldwide per month (Statista 2019). We categorize the threat of **data theft** in case of occurrence probability as medium, since in context of an ICU, the reason for cyberattacks is to harm people or extorting ransom by death threats. We do not rank it as low, because capturing sensitive information can be still profitable. The ENISA ranks the probability of device and data theft as 'a rare attack' in context of an entire hospital (Mayol et al. 2016). With ICUs almost only processing highly sensitive data, we rank the probability higher than for hospitals in general, due to the reward of the thief.

In result, the risk assessment shows a risk value of 'high' for all threats except **data theft**, which is ranked as 'medium'.

6   Conclusion

In this work, we presented a cybersecurity threat model specifically designed for a smart ICU network, establishing a connection between cybersecurity resilience and ICU resilience. Moreover, we conducted a risk analysis within an ICU context, assigning risk levels to various components.

Future research should delve deeper into risk analysis for each network component category. More sophisticated risk assessment models, such as the DREAD model (UcedaVelez and Morana 2015), could be adapted to quantify risks more thoroughly associated with cybersecurity threats in ICU networks. Additionally, a corresponding mitigation strategy should be developed and provided for each identified threat to the smart ICU network category.

References

Alomani, H., Alanzi, F., Alotaibi, Y.: System, Space, Staff, and Stuff framework in establishing a new pediatric critical care unit (PICU) (4S Framework) – ncbi.nlm.nih.gov (2022). https://www.ncbi.nlm.nih.gov/pmc/articles/PMC9668042/. Accessed 27 July 2023

Anderson, D., Jackson, A., Halpern, N.: Informatics for the modern intensive care unit. Crit. Care Nurs. Q. **41**, 60–67 (2018). https://doi.org/10.1097/CNQ.0000000000000186

Bullen, M., Hughes, T., Marshall, J.D.: The evolution of nice Medtech innovation briefings and their associated technologies. Value Health **20**, A595 (2017)

Cagnazzo, M., Hertlein, M., Holz, T., Pohlmann, N.: Threat modeling for mobile health systems. In: 2018 IEEE Wireless Communications and Networking Conference Workshops, WCNC 2018 Workshops, Barcelona, Spain, 15–18 April 2018, pp. 314–319. IEEE (2018). https://doi.org/10.1109/WCNCW.2018.8369033

Eliash, C., Lazar, I., Nissim, N.: SEC-C-U: the security of intensive care unit medical devices and their ecosystems. IEEE Access **PP**, 1 (2020). https://doi.org/10.1109/ACCESS.2020.2984726

ENISA: Risk Assessment Methodology (2017). https://www.enisa.europa.eu/risk-level-tool/methodology/. Accessed 26 July 2023

Hollnagel, E.: RAG - Resilience Analysis Grid (2015)

Kotz, D., Gunter, C.A., Kumar, S., Weiner, J.P.: Privacy and security in mobile health: a research agenda. Computer **49**(6), 22–30 (2016). https://doi.org/10.1109/MC.2016.185

Leidinger, C., Seelmann, V., Maasern, C.: Whitepaper: 5G - Evolution oder Revolution? (2020). https://www.fir.rwth-aachen.de/fileadmin/publikationen/whitepaper/cluster-whitepaper_5g.pdf

Lin, J.-C.: Synchronization requirements for 5G: an overview of standards and specifications for cellular networks. IEEE Veh. Technol. Mag. **13**(3), 91–99 (2018)

Mao, Z., Liu, C., Li, Q., Cui, Y., Zhou, F.: Intelligent intensive care unit: current and future trends. Intensive Care Res. **3** (2023). https://doi.org/10.1007/s44231-023-00036-5

Martínez-Pérez, B., De la Torre Díez, I., Lopez-Coronado, M.: Privacy and security in mobile health apps: a review and recommendations. J. Med. Syst. **39** (2014). https://doi.org/10.1007/s10916-014-0181-3

Mayol, J., et al.: Smart Hospitals Security and Resilience for Smart Health Service and Infrastructures, December 2016. https://doi.org/10.2824/28801

Mee, P., Brandenburg, R.: After reading, writing and arithmetic, the 4th 'r' of literacy is cyber-risk (2020). https://www.weforum.org/agenda/2020/12/cyber-risk-cyber-security-education. Accessed 28 July 2023

Peralta-Ochoa, A., Chaca-Asmal, P., Guerrero-Vásquez, L., Ordonez-Ordonez, J., Coronel-González, E.: Smart healthcare applications over 5G networks: a systematic review. Appl. Sci. **13**, 1469 (2023). https://doi.org/10.3390/app13031469

Plugmann, P.: Gibt es einen Rechtsanspruch auf mentale Unversehrtheit? Ideen für innovative Ansätze am Beispiel des Gesundheitswesens. In: Grinblat, R., Etterer, D., Plugmann, P. (eds.) Innovationen im Gesundheitswesen: Rechtliche und ökonomische Rahmenbedingungen und Potentiale, pp. 193–203. Springer Gabler, Wiesbaden (2022). https://doi.org/10.1007/978-3-658-33801-5_11

Salluh, J.I.F., Kurtz, P., Bastos, L.S.L., Quintairos, A., Zampieri, F.G., Bozza, F.A.: The resilient intensive care unit. Ann. Intens. Care (2022). https://doi.org/10.1186/s13613-022-01011-x

Statista: Number of electrical outages in firms in a typical month worldwide in 2018, by region (2019). https://www.statista.com/statistics/1069593/power-outages-firms-typical-month-global-by-region/. Accessed 27 July 2023

Tenzer, F.: Volumen der jährlich generierten/replizierten digitalen Datenmenge weltweit von 2010 bis 2022 und Prognose bis 2027 (in Zettabyte) (2023). https://de.statista.com/statistik/daten/studie/267974/umfrage/prognose-zum-weltweit-generierten-datenvolumen/

Tunder, R.: Market Access Management für Pharma-und Medizinprodukte. Instrumente, Verfahren und Erfolgsfaktoren: SpringerGabler, Wiesbaden (2020)

UcedaVelez, T., Morana, M.M.: Risk Centric Threat Modeling: Process for Attack Simulation and Threat Analysis, 1st edn. Wiley Publishing, Hoboken (2015). 0470500964

Winkelhake, U.: Die digitale Transformation der Automobilindustrie. Springer, Heidelberg (2017). https://doi.org/10.1007/978-3-662-54935-3

Characterizing Privacy Risks
in Healthcare IoT Systems

Shuai Li[1], Alessio Baiocco[2], and Shouhuai Xu[1(✉)]

[1] Department of Computer Science, University of Colorado Colorado Springs,
Colorado Springs, CO 80918, USA
{sli,sxu}@uccs.edu
[2] Department of Information Security and Communication Technology,
Norwegian University of Science and Technology NTNU, Gjøvik, Norway
alessio.baiocco@ntnu.no

Abstract. The advancement in Internet of Things (IoT) technology has been having a huge societal and economic impact, effectively changing the paradigms in doing business including the healthcare industry. While citizens now can enjoy the convenience brought up by healthcare IoT systems, such as wearable healthcare IoT devices, the privacy risks incurred by these systems and devices are not well understood, let alone adequately addressed. In this paper we systematically characterize the privacy risks in healthcare IoT systems, by considering a range of privacy attack vectors such as those that can be imposed by healthcare IoT device fingerprinting and semi-honest Internet Service Providers. Then, we leverage these characteristics to guide us in exploring countermeasures for mitigating privacy risks in healthcare IoT systems. We hope the present study will serve as a baseline for designing a systematic solution to protect citizen's privacy in healthcare IoT systems.

Keywords: Healthcare IoT Systems · Healthcare IoT Devices · Privacy · Data Breach · Privacy Risk · Cyber Risk

1 Introduction

Internet of Things (IoT) devices have become popular recent years, including smart watch and smart home ecosystem (e.g., smart thermostat, WiFi plug). Correspondingly, the healthcare industry has leveraged IoT devices to improve their services, leading to the notion of *healthcare IoT systems*, which have been widely employed for healthcare functions such as automated and remote patient monitoring, glucose monitoring, smart inhaler, and health data collection [21,30, 43,64]. This leads to a large amount of data that can not only be used by doctors for purposes such as diagnosing and immediate attention to health issues, but also be used for healthcare research purposes. It is predicted that the global market size of healthcare IoT devices will rapidly grow from US$291.2 billion in 2023 to US$861.3 billion in 2030 [1].

H. Abie et al. (Eds.): SUNRISE 2023, CCIS 1884, pp. 51–68, 2024.
https://doi.org/10.1007/978-3-031-55829-0_4

With the fast-growing popularity of healthcare IoT systems, we must adequately understand, characterize, and mitigate the potential security and privacy risks pertinent to healthcare IoT systems. For example, healthcare IoT devices are widely known to have unaddressed vulnerability surface that makes them susceptible to many attack vectors. This imposes a big risk because healthcare data often, if not always, include sensitive personal information, such as one's vital signs (e.g., pulse rate, body temperature) and medical problems (e.g., blood sugar level, blood pressures). These sensitive healthcare data pose a serious threat to citizens' privacy and potential unfair social welfare (e.g., a healthcare insurance company may refuse to sell insurance to a person when the company knows what kinds of medical problems from which the person is suffering).

To the best of our knowledge, the privacy problem in the context of healthcare IoT systems has not received the due amount of attention, meaning much research remains to be done. In this paper, we conduct a systematic study on characterizing the privacy risks in healthcare IoT systems.

Our Contributions. This paper makes two contributions. First, we characterize the privacy risks that can occur to healthcare IoT systems, through the following perspectives: (i) attack vectors via healthcare IoT device fingerprinting, (ii) attack vectors associated with Internet communications despite the employment of standard countermeasures such as cryptography-protected communications (e.g., Transport Layer Security or TLS, VPN-protected communications) and anonymous communication channels (e.g., Tor), (iii) attack vectors that are applicable to IoT data collection, (iv) attack vectors that may be waged by a curious or semi-honest Internet Service Provider (ISP), and (v) attack vectors that may be waged against healthcare service provider servers. Second, we leverage the resulting characteristics to guide our exploration of potential countermeasures to protect healthcare privacy against those attack vectors. This exploration would pave a way for future studies on designing systematic and practical solutions to harden healthcare privacy.

Related Works. Healthcare IoT techniques have shown great potential in providing high-quality healthcare services to citizens as evidenced by the following studies. Liu *et al.* [43] proposed an IoT-based heart ECG monitoring system that can detect cardiac abnormality in real time. Wu *et al.* [64] proposed to integrate ECG sensors into a T-shirt and use a bio-potential chip to collect quality ECG data. Istepanian *et al.* [30] reported a non-invasive IoT glucometer to monitor the glucose in real time. Fu and Liu [21] designed a non-invasive tissue oximeter to measure the blood oxygen saturation level, along with heart rate and pulse parameters.

However, the security and privacy issues in healthcare IoT systems have received much less attention and there are not so many studies. Tang *et al.* [62] designed a privacy-preserving healthcare data aggregation scheme that can achieve secure data collection from multiple sources and provide fair incentives for contributing patients. Fang *et al.* [19] proposed an anomaly detection scheme to detect healthcare IoT devices that have been compromised by attackers. Li *et al.* [37] adopted consortium blockchains to allow patients to manage, share, trade their medical records securely. In addition, there are early studies on analyzing risks associated with IoT systems in the healthcare domain [3] and there are some studies on exploring countermeasures [36,58,63]. For example, the Open Web Application Security Project (OWASP) [58] has identified some threats and vulnerabilities in healthcare IoT systems, including the lack of authorization, the insufficient authentication associated with the pertinent Internet communications, the insecure web interface of the healthcare service provider servers, the lack of transport layer encryption, the insecure network service, the insecure cloud interface, the inadequate security configuration, and the insecure mobile interface. Despite these studies, there is no systematic understanding on the privacy risks in healthcare IoT systems. For example, even [3] does not present a system model that would be comparable to what we will propose in this paper, which means that their analysis of risks would not be applicable to our setting. The present study aims at a systematic characterization of privacy risks. For example, we investigate privacy risks despite the employment of countermeasures that could have prevented some vulnerabilities discussed in [3] (e.g., employing sufficient authentication and transport layer cryptographic mechanisms).

Paper Organization. The rest of the paper is organized as follows. Section 2 presents the system model of healthcare IoT systems. Section 3 characterizes the privacy risks associated with healthcare IoT systems. Section 4 explores countermeasures to mitigate the privacy risks. Section 5 discusses the limitations of the present study. Section 6 concludes the paper with several exciting future research directions.

2   System Model

Figure 1 describes the system model of healthcare IoT systems, which will severe as the basis for discussing privacy risks in healthcare IoT systems and countermeasures for mitigating these privacy risks. We consider a range of healthcare IoT devices, including: emergency button (for emergency care), heart rate monitor, glucose monitor, sleep tracker, and blood sugar monitor. These devices are assumed to be connected to a gateway or a smartphone. The connection can be via WiFi, ZigBee, or Bluetooth Low Energy (BTLE).

The gateway is responsible for collecting data from those devices and communicating healthcare data to some healthcare servers by some healthcare service providers. There are multiple servers because the IoT devices are manufactured by different companies and each service provider has its own server to collect and analyze the data collected from its customers or patients. The analysis results are assumed to be returned back to a customer or patient via an App provided by the service provider, and the App runs in the gateway (i.e., smartphone). The communications between the gateway and the healthcare servers are based on the Internet, likely facilitated by some Internet Service Provider (ISP).

To protect the privacy of customers or patients, the healthcare servers often adopt some "standard" security and privacy mechanisms. For example, they

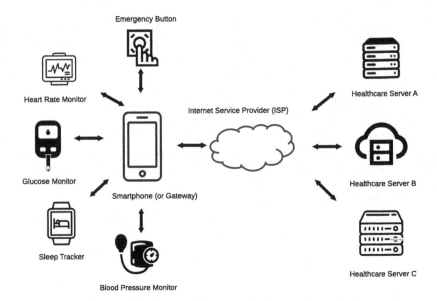

Fig. 1. System model of healthcare IoT systems

would employ the TLS protocol or the Virtual Private Network (VPN) technology to protect the communication between the gateway and the server in question. Moreover, this gateway-server communication may even be protected by some anonymous communication mechanisms, such as the Tor technology. At the application layer, a customer or patient may have created some pseudonym rather than using real name in the communication (e.g., for authenticating to a server), and a server may not know the mapping between the pseudonym and the real name of the customer or patient.

The research question we ask is: even if the aforementioned security and privacy mechanisms have been employed in healthcare IoT systems, is the privacy of customers or patients adequately protected? In what follows we characterize the privacy risks in healthcare IoT systems despite the employment of the standard security and privacy mechanisms mentioned above.

3   Privacy Risks in Healthcare IoT Systems

Due to the sensitive nature of the healthcare data, privacy protection in healthcare IoT systems is a necessity and required by law. In what follows we discuss six categories of privacy risks with respect to the system model presented above.

3.1   Privacy Risks Incurred by Communications Between Healthcare IoT Devices and the Gateway (Smartphone)

Healthcare IoT devices connect to the gateway via wireless communications, which provide the attackers the chance to eavesdrop the connection. Encrypting the traffic of healthcare IoT devices to the gateway can mitigate this risk, but encryption alone is far from sufficient because studies have showed that wireless devices could be fingerprinted by exploiting the identifiable features at the physical layer, the Medium Access Control (MAC) layer, and the network layer [69].

First, the imperfection in the manufacture process of wireless transmitters can cause varying wireless communication features (e.g., clock skew, frequency offset, and phase offset) [24]. As a consequence, healthcare IoT devices manufactured by the same vendor would share some common wireless features, which can be exploited by an attacker to recognize what IoT devices are being used and who are their vendors.

Second, some details of the MAC layer protocol are unspecified in the pertinent standard. As a consequence, the concrete implementation is largely left to the vendors and the discrepancy between these implementations can be exploited to infer the vendor to which a healthcare IoT device belongs [12].

Third, an attacker could exploit network-layer features to fingerprint healthcare IoT devices effectively [59]. This is because different kinds of IoT devices communicate with the gateway in different ways (e.g., the frequency of communication, the number of packets that are communicated). More specifically, network-layer features such as the number of packets, the packet size, and the direction of the packets can be exploited by an attacker to distinguish different kinds of healthcare IoT devices [38]. An even more concrete example is that the heart rate monitor may incur more frequent updates than the glucose monitor does, and this discrepancy can be exploited to tell these devices apart. This privacy risk cannot be prevented by encrypting the traffic because cryptosystems cannot hide the frequency of communications.

3.2   Privacy Risks Incurred by Internet Communications Despite Standard Countermeasures

Pertinent to the system model described in Fig. 1, there are privacy risks associated with the communications between the gateway and the healthcare service provider servers (or clouds), which would be partly or completely based on Internet. To characterize these risks, we consider three scenarios: the communications are protected by TLS; the communications are protected by VPN; the communications are protected by anonymous communication techniques such as Tor. We do not consider the scenario where none of these mechanisms (i.e., TLS, VPN, Tor) is employed because in which case a passive attacker can breach a user's privacy completely by eavesdropping the channel owing to the fact that the personal medical data is sent in plaintext.

Privacy Risks Despite TLS-protected Communications. In this scenario, the smartphone that acts as a gateway of the BWAN (Body Wide Area Network), which consists of the smartphone and the healthcare IoT devices (including their associated sensors), is expected to communicate securely with the healthcare service provider servers using the well-established TLS protocol. The TLS protocol provides, among other things, authentication, confidentiality, and data integrity services between two parties by establishing an authenticated private channel via an appropriate key-exchange procedure. That is, TLS allows mutual authentication between users' smartphones/gateways and the remote medical servers, encrypts data to assure it confidentiality, and assures that the data (encrypted or not) is not manipulated during transmission.

However, the employment of TLS might give a false sense of privacy protection, at least for the following four reasons. First, earlier versions of TLS (i.e., version 1.1 and version 1.2) are known to be vulnerable, explaining why TLS version 1.3 has been proposed. However, many computers or devices in the real world (smartphone and/or the server in this context) have not employed the most updated protocol [31,60], meaning that some of them would be susceptible to known attacks. Second, even if TLS version 1.3 is used, the authenticity of public key certificate of the gateway and/or the server represents another source of potential vulnerability even if these certificates are issued by trusted certification authority and their integrity is assured. One root cause of this phenomenon is that there are systems-based attacks against cryptosystems that may not be detected immediately, and these delays undermine the trustworthiness of cryptographic services owing to the presence of (for example) compromised cryptographic signing keys and/or functions [80]. Third, there are vulnerabilities that can affect the assurance offered by TLS, such as the CRIME attack [31] and the BREACH attack [22,31,49], which exploit the cookie mechanism by brute-forcing them. Fourth, TLS requires a granular configuration (application to application), which offers a great configuration flexibility but, if not properly managed, opens doors to serious implementation vulnerabilities that can be exploited by attackers [56].

Even if the preceding risks associated with TLS are carefully prevented, TLS does not provide any means to assure anonymous communications between a gateway and a healthcare service provider server. As a consequence, an attacker passively eavesdropping the Internet could easily figure out which user (via the user's smartphone) is communicating with which healthcare service provider, which could breach privacy. For example, if a user's smartphone often communicates with a cancer care service provider, this communication alone would expose that the user has the kind of cancer in question.

Privacy Risks Despite VPN-protected Communications. The VPN technology aims to create a secure point-to-point connection over the Internet (insecure network) between two networks or devices (e.g., the gateway and a healthcare service provider in the context of the present paper) [2]. By creating a point-to-point connection, the VPN technology encapsulates IP packets to prevent attackers from sniffing the network traffic. It can also prevent ISPs from spying on the network traffic of its users. In general, VPN can guarantee data integrity, confidentiality and authenticity of network communications.

Still, privacy risks can emerge despite the employment of the VPN technology for a gateway to access a healthcare service provider server. For example, when the VPN service is outsourced to an external service provider that handles the activities of its users, the VPN service provider can be a threat to privacy. Second, the cryptographic protocol that is used by a VPN may have vulnerabilities, such as those associated with the key exchange protocols whose cryptographic properties are extremely delicate. Such vulnerabilities could cause the compromise of data confidentiality, and thus privacy of the users. Third, the environment in which VPN is used can pose as a threat. This can be demonstrated by the LocalNet attack [81]. Putting this attack into the context of the present paper, a compromised router between a gateway and a healthcare service provider server can, despite the use of VPN, provide the client with incorrect network settings (e.g., routing tables), which represent public IP addresses of interest to the attackers as part of the local network. As a consequence, the data communicated in a VPN channel falls under the exclusions and bypasses the VPN tunnel [81].

Even if the preceding risks associated with VPNs are carefully prevented, VPN, similar to TLS, does not provide any means to assuring anonymous communication between a gateway and a healthcare service provider server. As a consequence, an attacker passively eavesdropping the Internet can still breach a user's privacy by monitoring communication patterns (e.g., what disease a user may be suffering as shown in the case of TLS).

Privacy Risks Despite Tor-protected Communications. Tor [13,38,55] is one implementation of the concept of Onion Routing. It is a network of virtual tunnels that aim to assure privacy and anonymity of its users by preventing passive attackers from tracking the traffic generated by, in the context of this paper, a gateway and a healthcare service provider server. While using cryptosystems to protect the confidentiality and integrity of the payload, Tor could give a false sense of privacy that it can hid the source-destination communication relationship because Tor is also vulnerable to attacks [13]. As one example, the *Autonomous System* eavesdropping attack [4] can be waged by the ISP used by a smartphone (i.e., gateway in this paper) to allow the autonomous system that deals with the re-routing of packets, to be present in the access relay and exit relay of the smartphone. As a consequence, the attacker can carry out a correlation attack between the incoming and outgoing traffic to breach privacy. As another example, the *exit node* eavesdropping attack [33] can be waged by its ISP to intercept the traffic from an exit Tor node. Since the exit relay traffic may not be encrypted by the Tor user and Tor doesn't encrypt the exit relay traffic by itself, the ISP may successfully eavesdrop the exit relay traffic.

3.3   Privacy Risks in Healthcare IoT Data Collection

Healthcare IoT devices leverage a smartphone as the gateway to communicate with a healthcare service provider server largely because of their constrained power and computational capability. Unfortunately, the gateway (smartphone) is subject to cyber attacks. For example, a smartphone often runs many apps, and a malicious app may be able to break its sandbox via privilege-escalation to control the smartphone and the other apps (e.g., healthcare apps). Moreover, the apps may share the smartphone's cache in the CPU, making cache side-channel attacks possible. For example, a malicious app that uses the same cache with a healthcare app can perform a side-channel attack (e.g., PRIME+PROBE [50]) to learn how the cache has been affected by the healthcare app, effectively inferring the activities of the healthcare app and even its cryptographic private keys. In addition, studies (e.g., [65]) even showed that an attacker can exploit inaudible attacks to compromise a smartphone (e.g., sending unauthorized text messages, triggering malicious downloads, changing the WiFi settings, or performing context-aware voice recording). As a consequence, the attacker can exploit these attacks to breach private healthcare data.

3.4   Privacy Risks Incurred by Curious Internet Service Providers

It is important to highlight a particular privacy threat vector that can be waged by ISPs, including the scenarios that an ISP itself is compromised and then abused to breach the privacy of its users. Healthcare IoT device users typically depend on ISPs to connect to healthcare care service provider servers. However, an ISP can be curious (i.e., semi-honest) to learn its users' usage of healthcare IoT devices. In what follows we discuss why standard techniques for privacy protection are not adequate.

- **TLS**. TLS can protect the communications between users' smart-phones/gateways and the healthcare service provider servers, but not the communications between the healthcare IoT devices and the associated smart-phone/gateway in most cases (owing to the computational and communication overhead incurred by TLS). Although employing TLS can prevent an ISP from learning the application-layer data, it cannot prevent the ISP from learning "who is communicating with whom" or "which IP address is communicating with which other IP address." This can breach the privacy of the users. For example, if a user frequently communicates with a healthcare service provider offering cancer therapy, the ISP can infer that the user might be suffering from a cancer.
- **VPN**. The healthcare IoT gateway may use the VPN technology to communicate with a healthcare service provider server. In this case, the gateway would incur Internet communication traffic with the VPN server offered by the healthcare service provider, which still exposes with which healthcare service provider a user is communicating. Moreover, an ISP could exploit the traffic correlation technique to figure out the destination of the traffic originating from the gateway [32].
- **Tor**. As discussed above, Tor [13] can hide the communication relationship between a user and a healthcare service provider server to some extent. However, studies [38,59] have showed that traffic features, such as packet count and packet direction, could still leak information about the source and destination of the connection. In particular, privacy risk can be incurred when the Tor routers belong to a single ISP.

The preceding analysis shows that standard techniques cannot adequately prevent ISPs from breaching the privacy of users in healthcare IoT systems.

3.5   Privacy Risks Incurred by Attacks Against Healthcare Service Provider Servers

The healthcare service provider servers can become the target of cyberattacks. Recent years have witnessed some large-scale data leakage from healthcare servers, impacting millions of patients [20, 34, 67]. The leaked information include patient name, home address, date of birth, and appointment information. One approach to mitigating the privacy risks incurred by attacks against the healthcare service provider servers is to make these servers store personal information as little as possible. However, this is not practical for at least two reasons: (i) the healthcare service providers would treat the user's data as their assets; (ii) keeping all data pertinent to a user would enable a better healthcare service to the user because a complete medical history is a critical source of information when a user gets a serious disease.

3.6   Privacy Risks Despite the Use of Application-Layer Pseudonyms

One may suggest to use application-layer pseudonyms to alleviate privacy risks against a malicious or compromised healthcare service provider server and the other attacks mentioned above. For example, a user may use a pseudonym rather than personal identifier to index their healthcare data. However, this technique is often vulnerable to the re-identification attack because it cannot guarantee complete anonymity (e.g., the data may retain some "fingerprints" or "linkability" that can be exploited to recover the identity of a data owner [9, 54]). These deanonymization attacks may be waged by a malicious healthcare service provider, or by an attacker that compromised a healthcare service provider server.

To be more specific, we note that patient re-identification has been reported by correlating medical data saved in data servers with patient discharge logs [82]. It is intuitive that the greater the medical details of the pathology categorized with codes in the databases, the greater the possibility that this data will be re-identified. Moreover, the greater the side information made public by healthcare facilities, the greater the ability to deanonymize patient data by correlating them (e.g., information about hospitalizations and medical conditions, including prescription data, medical mailing lists , employers, debtors, friends, and family).

Note that making a user to have multiple pseudonyms is no good idea because it will reduce the usefulness of the healthcare data as a medical doctor cannot see the complete medical history of a patient and the statistical analysis conducted by a medical researcher would not obtain high-quality results.

4   Exploring Countermeasures for Enhancing Privacy in Healthcare IoT Systems

As analyzed above, privacy risks impose challenges that demand new solutions. In this section we explore four kinds of countermeasures that would be needed in order to mitigate those privacy risks.

4.1 Traffic Feature Obfuscation Between IoT Devices and Gateway

In order to defeat the healthcare IoT device fingerprinting attacks discussed above, we propose obfuscating the identifiable features at the physical layer, the MAC layer, and the network layer.

Fingerprint Obfuscation at the Physical Layer. The imperfection in the manufacture process of wireless transmitters is inevitable, which makes fingerprinting possible. One approach to alleviating the risk would be to make the physical layer's features device-specific rather than vendor-specific. The intuition is that if the physical-layer features of a healthcare IoT device are unique to the device and do not leak any information about its vendor, it would prevent an attacker from inferring the vendor. What remains to be investigated include: (i) the unique features could be exploited to unambiguously identify a device, which may have another kind of privacy implication because unique fingerprint may serve as a unique identifier of the device; (ii) how the manufacturing process may be "randomized" to achieve fingerprint obfuscation; and (iii) the required distance to the patient that makes the fingerprinting attacks feasible.

Fingerprint Obfuscation at the MAC Layer. MAC-layer features are incurred by vendor-specific implementations of the protocols when dealing with the unspecified details of MAC-layer protocols. To prevent the vendor-specific features at the MAC layer, a vendor should adopt more common implementation shared with other vendors, instead of crafting its own. To achieve this, the healthcare IoT industry should standardize the unspecified MAC layer details so as to preserve the healthcare IoT users' privacy at the MAC layer.

Fingerprint Obfuscation at the Network Layer. When a healthcare IoT device user is in a public space, an attacker can monitor its wireless traffic to learn the IoT devices that are being used. The network-layer features include packet size, packet count, packet directions, and burst pattern. To defeat such attacks, we propose obfuscating the network traffic features. In what follows we propose two preliminary schemes for this purpose.

- **Random Dummy Packet Injection.** When a healthcare IoT device communicates with the gateway (smartphone), both sides need to inject dummy packets randomly so as to obfuscate traffic features such as packet counts and packet direction. In order to prevent interference to the existing IoT data processing services, an IoT device should send its real packets with no delay, while injecting dummy packets to the gateway with a pre-determined probability p_i. Similarly, the gateway sends its real packets to the IoT device as usual, while sending dummy packets with a probability p_g. To better protect user privacy, we prefer larger p_i and p_g. However, the IoT devices are usually energy-constrained, which means that p_i should not be too large; otherwise, the IoT device's power would be drained quickly. Thus, we need to make a trade-off when determining probability p_i. On the contrary, the gateway has no such constraints, and we can choose a larger p_g to achieve better privacy protection.

– **Random Packet Padding.** If the packets sent by the healthcare IoT devices and the gateway have different sizes, we propose padding the packets in order to prevent the packet size from leaking any information to the attacker. When an IoT device or the gateway is about to send a packet with size s_c, the sender should pad the packet to the size $s_c + d$ with a probability p_c, where d is a random integer between 0 and $s_{max} - s_c$ and s_{max} is the maximum size a packet is allowed to have.

Note that the general idea of traffic padding has been proposed in other context [35], but hasn't been systematically studied in medical IoT settings. Open research questions include: How can we determine the padding parameters for medical IoT devices? Moreover, these techniques should be used together with cryptographic mechanisms for encrypting the content of device-gateway communication; otherwise, an attacker could recognize the dummy packets. For this purpose, light-weight cryptosystems, including both confidentiality and integrity protection mechanisms, should be used.

4.2 Privacy Enhancement for Healthcare IoT Device Data Collection

We propose taking countermeasures to defeat an attacker from learning healthcare data from the gateway or smartphone. In response to a malicious app taking control of the smartphone or gateway, we advocate adopting the Trusted Execution Environment (TEE) and implement the healthcare apps to leverage TEE [18]. This assures that even if a process with a higher privilege has been hijacked by a malicious app, the attacker still cannot compromise the data of the healthcare app because the data is encrypted in the memory space. Note that it is only when the healthcare app gets executed, the data is decrypted in the TEE. In addition, we need to address the cache side-channel attacks by run-time diversification or cache partitioning [42], so that a malicious app and healthcare app do not share a common cache resource.

4.3 Thwarting a Curious ISP

We propose addressing the privacy risks that can be incurred by a curious ISP by hiding the true destination of the gateway's Internet traffic. TLS protocol cannot conceal the true destination's IP address, while VPN service is subject to the traffic correlation attack mentioned above. Therefore, we propose adopting the onion routing [55] or the TOT implementation to conceal the true destination of the gateway's traffic, but in a more sophisticated way than the standard use described in Sect. 3.4, by using onion routers that belong to different ISPs. Recall that Tor contains thousands of volunteer nodes or onion routers. We propose that the gateway (smartphone) should choose at least three onion routers as its *entry guard, middle relay,* and *exit relay.* A gateway should have its traffic to go through the chosen onion routers sequentially before reaching the healthcare service provider server. The gateway exhibits traffic destined to the Tor onion routers such that a curious ISP has no idea about the true destination. It's also much harder to conduct traffic correlation attacks on Tor onion routers as long as the three onion routers belong to different ISPs (i.e., no single ISP can monitor these three onion routers).

Note that recent studies [38,59] find that the traffic features of Tor networks can be informative, and that an advanced attacker can harvest these traffic features to tell which website a Tor user has visited. In our context, such an attack can be exploited by a curious ISP to learn which healthcare service provider server the gateway has connected to, which compromises the user's privacy. In order to mitigate this attack, we propose that the gateway should initiate deliberate web browsing activities when connecting to the healthcare service provider server, and both the web browsing traffic and IoT traffic use the same set of onion routers. The goal is to mix the two kinds of traffic together so that the traffic features of healthcare IoT devices will be obfuscated by the web browsing traffic.

4.4   Data Privacy Protection for Healthcare Provider Server

Healthcare service provider servers can become the subject of the cyber attacks discussed above. Although the stored medical records in the these servers may be anonymized, the records are still subject to re-identification attacks. To protect data privacy, we propose the following scheme. First, the data should be encrypted using some appropriate homomorphic encryption schemes that allow the desired operations over ciphertexts corresponding to some applications (e.g., statistical analysis). Second, the private key for decrypting the data and the ciphertext resulting from homomorphic operations over the ciphertexts should be protected in a secure environment, such as TEE such that the private key cannot be compromised (assuming the attacker cannot exploit any side-channel). However, one must recognize that even if the private key cannot be compromised, data privacy can still be at risk. This is because the cryptographic function corresponding to the private key could be compromised without compromising the private key. In theory this is known as *oracle access* to the cryptographic function (e.g., decryption or digital signing). In practice, this threat has inspired many studies to mitigate the problem, such as [11,14,15,28,52,72,80].

5   Limitations

The present study has three limitations, which need to be addressed in future studies. First, the system model we considered, which focused on data collection, can be extended to accommodate other emerging components, such as edge computers with which the gateway may communicate with. Second, the extended system model may introduce new threat vectors, meaning that the threat model may need to be revised correspondingly. Third, we proposes several countermeasures to address the privacy risks but without experimental evaluation. The high-level design we proposed need to be elaborated, refined, and evaluated.

6   Conclusion and Future Research Directions

We have presented a characterization of privacy risks associated with healthcare IoT systems via a range of privacy attack vectors. We have explored counter-measures to mitigate these privacy risks. We hope this study will inspire many future endeavors on adequately assuring privacy in healthcare IoT systems.

Open problems for future studies are abundant. In addition to addressing the limitations mentioned above, we highlight the following.

First, how should we design a systematic architecture to assure privacy in healthcare IoT systems? This architecture should be holistic in the sense of encompassing all the layers, including the application layer and communication layer, because the preceding discussion suggests that privacy breaching can be achieved by exploiting information gathered at multiple layers.

Second, how should we design a systematic set of privacy-protection mechanisms to mitigate privacy risks in healthcare IoT systems? Similarly, the mechanisms should consider multiple layers and the inference attacks that may be waged by attackers. This is nontrivial because the current research are often geared towards point solutions. For example, cryptographic multiparty computation [23], an elegant mechanism for protecting data privacy when multiple participants need to conduct some joint computational tasks over the union of their data, does not prevent an eavesdropper to infer which participants are conducting such activities with which other participants. This means that additional mechanisms are needed in order to prevent the eavesdropped from making such inferences.

Third, how should we quantify privacy risks in healthcare IoT systems? How should we quantify the effectiveness or capabilities of each privacy mechanisms? What privacy metrics are needed? Although there have been some very nice and useful privacy metrics, such as differential privacy [17], we observe they are geared towards the application layer if not a particular kind of applications. As mentioned above, privacy risks can be incurred by exploiting information collected at different layers (e.g., application layer and communication layer). This highlights that privacy is an emergent property, which suggests that holistic privacy cannot be achieved by composing building-block or point solutions each of which achieves certain privacy assurances in their respective models [70].

Fourth, the preceding discussion suggests that privacy in the healthcare sector (and perhaps in a broader context) should be treated holistically. This is reminiscent of the notion of *cybersecurity dynamics* [71,76,77], which intends to model, quantify, and analyze cybersecurity from a holistic perspective because cybersecurity also exhibit emergent behavior [8,53,70,78]. This prompts us to envision the notion of *privacy dynamics*, which intuitively means the following: the degree of privacy breached by the adversary evolves with time, and there could be a threshold of tolerable privacy reach above which the privacy in question is completely breached. This means that privacy breaching would exhibit the *phase transition* phenomenon, which has been exhibited by theoretical cybersecurity dynamics studies [10,25,26,39,41,45,51,66,68,73–75,79,83,84] and data-driven cybersecurity studies [6,7,27,61]. For example, it would be very interesting to know whether the rich phenomena exhibited by cybersecurity dynamics would be exhibited by privacy dynamics as well, such as: global convergence [84] and global attractivity [26] for preventive and reactive cyber defense dynamics, and chaos for active cyber defense dynamics under certain circumstances [83]. The privacy implications of these phenomena would also deserve investigation. Moreover, we would need to define privacy metrics to accommodate the emergent properties, reminiscent of studies on defining cybersecurity metrics to measuring cybersecurity from a holistic perspective [5, 8, 16, 46, 53, 78].

Fifth. going beyond the healthcare sector, it is important to realize that cyber attackers are interested in compromising healthcare data (e.g., via cyber social engineering attacks [44, 47, 48, 57]) not only for the purpose of breaching privacy, but also for garnering patients' information and then exploiting the breached data to wage further attacks (e.g., blackmailing) [29, 40].

Acknowledgement. We thank the anonymous reviewers for their useful comments. Shouhuai Xu is supported in part by NSF Grant #2115134 and Colorado State Bill 18–086. This research work is also a contribution to the International Alliance for Strengthening Cybersecurity and Privacy in Healthcare (CybAlliance, Project no. 337316).

References

1. Internet of things in healthcare market size report (2030). https://www.grandviewresearch.com/industry-analysis/internet-of-things-iot-healthcare-market

2. Abbas, H., et al.: Security assessment and evaluation of VPNs: a comprehensive survey. ACM Comput. Surv. **55**(13s), 1–47 (2023)

3. Abouzakhar, N.S., Jones, A., Angelopoulou, O.: Internet of things security: a review of risks and threats to healthcare sector. In: 2017 IEEE International Conference on Internet of Things (iThings) and IEEE Green Computing and Communications (GreenCom) and IEEE Cyber, Physical and Social Computing (CPSCom) and IEEE Smart Data (SmartData), pp. 373–378, June 2017

4. Akhoondi, M., Yu, C., Madhyastha, H.: Lastor: a low-latency as-aware tor client. In 2012 IEEE Symposium on Security and Privacy, pp. 476–490 (2012)

5. Charlton, J., Du, P., Xu, S.: A new method for inferring ground-truth labels and malware detector effectiveness metrics. In: Lu, W., Sun, K., Yung, M., Liu, F. (eds.) SciSec 2021. LNCS, vol. 13005, pp. 77–92. Springer, Cham (2021). https://doi.org/10.1007/978-3-030-89137-4_6

6. Chen, H., Cho, J., Xu, S.: Quantifying the security effectiveness of firewalls and dmzs. In: Proceedings of HoTSoS 2018, pp. 9:1–9:11 (2018)

7. Chen, H., Cam, H., Xu, S.: Quantifying cybersecurity effectiveness of dynamic network diversity. IEEE Trans. Dependable Secure Comput. **19**(6), 3804–3821 (2021)

8. Cho, J.H., Xu, S., Hurley, P.M., Mackay, M., Benjamin, T., Beaumont, M.: Stram: measuring the trustworthiness of computer-based systems. ACM Comput. Surv. **51**(6), 128:1–128:47 (2019)

9. Crețu, A., Monti, F., Marrone, S., Dong, X., Bronstein, M., Montjoye, Y.: Interaction data are identifiable even across long periods of time. Nat. Commun. **13**, 01 (2022)

10. Da, G., Xu, M., Xu, S.: A new approach to modeling and analyzing security of networked systems. In Proceedings of HotSoS 2014, pp. 6:1–6:12 (2014)
11. Dai, W., Parker, P., Jin, H., Xu, S.: Enhancing data trustworthiness via assured digital signing. IEEE TDSC **9**(6), 838–851 (2012)
12. Desmond, L., Yuan, C., Pheng, T., Lee, R.: Identifying unique devices through wireless fingerprinting. In: Proceedings of ACM WiSec, pp. 46–55 (2008)
13. Dingledine, R., Mathewson, N., Syverson, P.: Tor: the second-generation onion router. Proc. Usenix Security **4**, 303–320 (2004)
14. Dodis, Y., Katz, J., Xu, S., Yung, M.: Key-insulated public key cryptosystems. In: Knudsen, L.R. (ed.) EUROCRYPT 2002. LNCS, vol. 2332, pp. 65–82. Springer, Heidelberg (2002). https://doi.org/10.1007/3-540-46035-7_5
15. Dodis, Y., Katz, J., Xu, S., Yung, M.: Strong key-insulated signature schemes. In: Public Key Cryptography (PKC 2003), pp. 130–144 (2003)
16. Du, P., Sun, Z., Chen, H., Cho, J.H., Xu, S.: Statistical estimation of malware detection metrics in the absence of ground truth. IEEE T-IFS **13**(12), 2965–2980 (2018)
17. Dwork, C.: Differential privacy. In: Proceedings of Automata, Languages and Programming, 33rd International Colloquium (ICALP 2006), pp. 1–12 (2006)
18. Ekberg, J.E., Kostiainen, K., Asokan, N.: Trusted execution environments on mobile devices. In Proceedings of ACM CCS 2013, pp. 1497–1498 (2013)
19. Fang, L., Li, Y., Liu, Z., Yin, C., Li, M., Cao, Z.: A practical model based on anomaly detection for protecting medical IoT control services against external attacks. IEEE Trans. Ind. Inf. **17**(6), 4260–4269 (2020)
20. Fang, Z., Xu, M., Xu, S., Hu, T.: A framework for predicting data breach risk: leveraging dependence to cope with sparsity. IEEE Trans. Inf. Forensics Secur. **16**, 2186–2201 (2021)
21. Yu, F., Liu, J.: System design for wearable blood oxygen saturation and pulse measurement device. Procedia Manuf. **3**, 1187–1194 (2015)
22. Gluck, Y., Harris, N., Prado, A.: Breach: reviving the crime attack. Unpublished manuscript (2013)
23. Goldreich, O., Micali, S., Wigderson, A.: How to play any mental game or a completeness theorem for protocols with honest majority. In Proceedings of 19th ACM Symposium on Theory of Computing, pp. 218–229. ACM (1987)
24. Hall, J., Barbeau, M., Kranakis, E., et al.: Enhancing intrusion detection in wireless networks using radio frequency fingerprinting. Commun. Internet Inf. Technol. 201–206 (2004)
25. Han, Y., Lu, W., Xu, S.: Characterizing the power of moving target defense via cyber epidemic dynamics. In: HotSoS, pp. 1–12 (2014)
26. Han, Y., Lu, W., Xu, S.: Preventive and reactive cyber defense dynamics with ergodic time-dependent parameters is globally attractive. IEEE TNSE **8**(3), 2517–2532 (2021)
27. Harang, R.E., Kott, A.: Burstiness of intrusion detection process: Empirical evidence and a modeling approach. IEEE Trans. Inf. Forensics Secur. **12**(10), 2348–2359 (2017)
28. Harrison, K., Xu, S.: Protecting cryptographic keys from memory disclosures. In: IEEE/IFIP DSN 2007, pp. 137–143 (2007)
29. Hijji, M., Alam, G.: A multivocal literature review on growing social engineering based cyber-attacks/threats during the covid-19 pandemic: challenges and prospective solutions. IEEE Access **9**, 7152–7169 (2021)

30. Istepanian, R., Hu, S., Philip, N., Sungoor, A.: The potential of internet of m-health things "m-IoT" for non-invasive glucose level sensing. In: 2011 IEEE Conference of Engineering in Medicine and Biology Society, pp. 5264–5266 (2011)

31. Ivanov, O., Ruzhentsev, V., Oliynykov, R.: Comparison of modern network attacks on TLS protocol. In: 2018 IEEE International Conference Problems of Infocommunications. Science and Technology, pp. 565–570 (2018)

32. Johnson, A., Wacek, C., Jansen, R., Sherr, M., Syverson, P.: Users get routed: traffic correlation on tor by realistic adversaries. In: Proceedings of ACM CCS 2013, pp. 337–348 (2013)

33. Jonsson, T., Edeby, G.: Collecting and analyzing tor exit node traffic. MS Thesis, Blekinge Institute of Technology (2021)

34. The HIPPA Journal. Healthcare data breach statistics. https://www.hipaajournal.com/healthcare-data-breach-statistics/

35. Juárez, M., Imani, M., Perry, M., Dıaz, C., Wright, M.: Wtf-pad: toward an efficient website fingerprinting defense for tor. In: Proceedings of ESORICS (2016)

36. Krutz, R.L., Vines, R.D.: Cloud security: a comprehensive guide to secure cloud computing wiley publishing. Inc., Indianapolis, Indiana (2010)

37. Li, C., Dong, M., Li, J., Gang, X., Chen, X., Ota, K.: Healthchain: Secure EMRs management and trading in distributed healthcare service system. IEEE Internet Things J. $8(9)$, 7192–7202 (2021)

38. Li, S., Guo, H., Hopper, N.: Measuring information leakage in website fingerprinting attacks and defenses. In: Proceedings of ACM CCS 2018, pp. 1977–1992 (2018)

39. Li, X., Parker, P., Xu, S.: A stochastic model for quantitative security analyses of networked systems. IEEE TDSC $8(1)$, 28–43 (2011)

40. Lin, T., et al.: Susceptibility to spear-phishing emails: effects of internet user demographics and email content. ACM Trans. Comput.-Hum. Interact. (TOCHI) $26(5)$, 1–28 (2019)

41. Lin, Z., Lu, W., Xu, S.: Unified preventive and reactive cyber defense dynamics is still globally convergent. IEEE/ACM ToN $27(3)$, 1098–1111 (2019)

42. Liu, F., Yarom, Y., Ge, Q., Heiser, G., Lee, R.B.: Last-level cache side-channel attacks are practical. In: 2015 IEEE Symposium on Security and Privacy, pp. 605–622 (2015)

43. Liu, M.-L., Tao, L., Yan, Z.: Internet of things-based electrocardiogram monitoring system. Chin. Patent $102(764)$, 118 (2012)

44. Longtchi, T., Rodriguez, R., Al-Shawaf, L., Atyabi, A., Xu, S.: Why have defenses against social engineering attacks achieved limited success? CoRR (2022)

45. Lu, W., Xu, S., Yi, X.: Optimizing active cyber defense. In: Das, S.K., Nita-Rotaru, C., Kantarcioglu, M. (eds.) GameSec 2013. LNCS, vol. 8252, pp. 206–225. Springer, Cham (2013). https://doi.org/10.1007/978-3-319-02786-9_13

46. Mireles, J., Ficke, E., Cho, J., Hurley, P., Xu, S.: Metrics towards measuring cyber agility. IEEE Trans. Inf. Forensics Secur. $14(12)$, 3217–3232 (2019)

47. Montañez, R., Atyabi, A., Xu, S.: Book Chapter in "Cybersecurity and Cognitive Science", chapter Social Engineering Attacks and Defenses in the Physical World vs. Cyberspace: A Contrast Study. Elsevier (2022)

48. Montañez, R., Golob, E., Shouhuai, X.: Human cognition through the lens of social engineering cyberattacks. Front. Psychol. 11, 1755 (2020)

49. Christopher Ng. Ssl-tls security flaws: the breach and logjam attacks. NTU Technical Report (2021)

50. Osvik, D.A., Shamir, A., Tromer, E.: Cache attacks and countermeasures: the case of AES. In: Pointcheval, D. (ed.) CT-RSA 2006. LNCS, vol. 3860, pp. 1–20. Springer, Heidelberg (2006). https://doi.org/10.1007/11605805_1

51. Paarporn, K., Brown, P.N., Xu, S.: Analysis of contagion dynamics with active cyber defenders. CoRR (2023)
52. Parker, T.P., Xu, S.: A method for safekeeping cryptographic keys from memory disclosure attacks. In: Chen, L., Yung, M. (eds.) INTRUST 2009. LNCS, vol. 6163, pp. 39–59. Springer, Heidelberg (2010). https://doi.org/10.1007/978-3-642-14597-1_3
53. Pendleton, M., Garcia-Lebron, R., Cho, J.H., Xu, S.: A survey on systems security metrics. ACM Comput. Surv. **49**(4), 62:1–62:35 (2016)
54. Powar, J., Beresford, A.R.: Sok: managing risks of linkage attacks on data privacy. Proc. Priv. Enhancing Technol. **2**, 97–116 (2023)
55. Reed, M.G., Syverson, P.F., Goldschlag, D.M.: Anonymous connections and onion routing. IEEE J. Sel. Areas Commun. **16**(4), 482–494 (1998)
56. Ristic, I.: Bulletproof SSL and TLS: understanding and deploying SSL/TLS and PKI to secure servers and web applications (2013)
57. Rodriguez, R.M., Xu, S.: Cyber social engineering kill chain. In: Proceedings of International Conference on Science of Cyber Security (SciSec 2022) (2022)
58. Shahid, J., Ahmad, R., Kiani, A., Ahmad, T., Saeed, S., Almuhaideb, A.: Data protection and privacy of the internet of healthcare things (IoHTs). Appl. Sci. **12**(4), 1927 (2022)
59. Sirinam, P., Mathews, N., Rahman, M.S., Wright, M.: Triplet fingerprinting: more practical and portable website fingerprinting with n-shot learning. In: Proceedings of 2019 ACM CCS, pp. 1131–1148 (2019)
60. Sirohi, P., Agarwal, A., Tyagi, S.: A comprehensive study on security attacks on SSL/TLS protocol. In: 2016 2nd International Conference on Next Generation Computing Technologies (NGCT), pp. 893–898. IEEE (2016)
61. Sun, Z., Xu, M., Schweitzer, K.M., Bateman, R.M., Kott, A., Xu, S.: Cyber attacks against enterprise networks: characterization, modeling and forecasting. In: Proceedings of SciSec 2023 (2023)
62. Wenjuan Tang, J., Ren, K.D., Zhang, Y.: Secure data aggregation of lightweight e-healthcare IoT devices with fair incentives. IEEE Internet Things J. **6**(5), 8714–8726 (2019)
63. Winkler, V.J.: Securing the Cloud: Cloud computer Security techniques and tactics. Elsevier (2011)
64. Wu, T., Redouté, J.-M., Yuce, M.: A wearable, low-power, real-time ECG monitor for smart T-shirt and IoT healthcare applications. In: Fortino, G., Wang, Z. (eds.) Advances in Body Area Networks I. IT, pp. 165–173. Springer, Cham (2019). https://doi.org/10.1007/978-3-030-02819-0_13
65. Xia, Q., Chen, Q., Xu, S.: Near-ultrasound inaudible trojan (Nuit): exploiting your speaker to attack your microphone. In: Calandrino, J.A., Troncoso, C. (eds.), Proceedings of Usenix Security (2023)
66. Xu, M., Da, G., Xu, S.: Cyber epidemic models with dependences. Internet Math. **11**(1), 62–92 (2015)
67. Xu, M., Schweitzer, K., Bateman, R., Xu, S.: Modeling and predicting cyber hacking breaches. IEEE Trans. Inf. Forensics Secur. **13**(11), 2856–2871 (2018)
68. Xu, M., Xu, S.: An extended stochastic model for quantitative security analysis of networked systems. Internet Math. **8**(3), 288–320 (2012)
69. Xu, Q., Zheng, R., Saad, W., Han, Z.: Device fingerprinting in wireless networks: challenges and opportunities. IEEE Commun. Surv. Tutorials **18**(1), 94–104 (2016)
70. Xu, S.: Emergent behavior in cybersecurity. In Proceedings of HotSoS, pp. 13:1–13:2 (2014)

71. Xu, S.: The cybersecurity dynamics way of thinking and landscape (invited paper). In: ACM Workshop on Moving Target Defense (2020)
72. Xu, S., Li, X., Parker, T., Wang, X.: Exploiting trust-based social networks for distributed protection of sensitive data. IEEE T-IFS **6**(1), 39–52 (2011)
73. Xu, S., Lu, W., Xu, L.: Push- and pull-based epidemic spreading in networks: thresholds and deeper insights. ACM TAAS **7**(3), 1–26 (2012)
74. Xu, S., Lu, W., Xu, L., Zhan, Z.: Adaptive epidemic dynamics in networks: thresholds and control. ACM TAAS **8**(4), 1–19 (2014)
75. Xu, S., Lu, W., Zhan, Z.: A stochastic model of multivirus dynamics. IEEE Trans. Dependable Secure Comput. **9**(1), 30–45 (2012)
76. Xu, S.: Cybersecurity dynamics. In: Proceedings of Symposium on the Science of Security (HotSoS 2014), pp. 14:1–14:2 (2014)
77. Xu, S.: Cybersecurity dynamics: a foundation for the science of cybersecurity. In: Wang, C., Lu, Z. (eds.) Proactive and Dynamic Network Defense, vol. 74, pp. 1–31. Springer, Cham (2019). https://doi.org/10.1007/978-3-030-10597-6_1
78. Xu, S.: Sarr: a cybersecurity metrics and quantification framework. In: Third International Conference on Science of Cyber Security (SciSec 2021), pp. 3–17 (2021)
79. Xu, S., Lu, W., Li, H.: A stochastic model of active cyber defense dynamics. Internet Math. **11**(1), 23–61 (2015)
80. Xu, S., Yung, M.: Expecting the unexpected: towards robust credential infrastructure. In: Dingledine, R., Golle, P. (eds.) FC 2009. LNCS, vol. 5628, pp. 201–221. Springer, Heidelberg (2009). https://doi.org/10.1007/978-3-642-03549-4_12
81. Xue, N., Malla, Y., Xia, Z., Pöpper, C., Vanhoef, M.: Bypassing tunnels: leaking {VPN} client traffic by abusing routing tables. In: Proceedings of Usenix Security, pp. 5719–5736 (2023)
82. Yoo, J.S., Thaler, A., Sweeney, L., Zang, J.: Risks to patient privacy: a re-identification of patients in maine and vermont statewide hospital data. J. Technol. Sci. **2018100901**, 1–62 (2018)
83. Zheng, R., Lu, W., Xu, S.: Active cyber defense dynamics exhibiting rich phenomena. In: Proceedings of HotSoS (2015)
84. Zheng, R., Lu, W., Xu, S.: Preventive and reactive cyber defense dynamics is globally stable. IEEE TNSE **5**(2), 156–170 (2018)

Invited Papers from Keynotes

Data Analytics, Digital Transformation, and Cybersecurity Perspectives in Healthcare

Kousik Barik[1], Sanjay Misra[2](✉), Sabarathinam Chockalingam[3], and Mario Hoffmann[2]

[1] Department of Computer Science, University of Alcala, Alcalá de Henares, Spain
kousik.kousik@edu.uah.es

[2] Department of Applied Data Science, Institute for Energy Technology, Halden, Norway
{Sanjay.Misra,Mario.Hoffmann}@ife.no

[3] Department of Risk and Security, Institute for Energy Technology, Halden, Norway
Sabarathinam.Chockalingam@ife.no

Abstract. Data analytics personalize treatments and improve outcomes in a fast-changing digital world. The infusion of digital technologies into healthcare processes and workflows offers enhancements in areas such as flexibility, scalability, reliability, agility, cost-effectiveness, and the overall quality of healthcare services and operations. However, the heightened dependence on these digital advancements underscores the imperative for robust cybersecurity measures. Safeguarding patient data, healthcare systems, and infrastructure from potential cyber threats becomes paramount in ensuring the integrity and security of the healthcare ecosystem. This study addresses data security concerns in the health organization, a digital health system. This study aims to explore the connections between interdependence, uncertainty, knowledge, and security in the digital transformation of healthcare organizations. The data is collected from healthcare organization managers' responses based on a questionnaire. The gathered data is used to test six hypotheses. A comprehensive questionnaire with Likert-scale responses serves as our research instrument. Furthermore, SmartPLS is used for statistical analysis and validating structural and measurement frameworks. Path coefficients and bootstrap confidence intervals support the hypothesis that digital uncertainty understanding improves interdependence, cybersecurity, and digital transformation. The findings indicate a strong positive relation between the healthcare organization's understanding of interdependence, uncertainty, and cybersecurity knowledge and its expenditures in cybersecurity solutions. This analysis shows that hypotheses H1, H3, and H4 significantly impact digital transformation security layers, with the greatest values (0.542), offering policymakers important information for improving digital resilience.

Keywords: Cyber resilience · Data analytics · Digital Transformation · Healthcare

H. Abie et al. (Eds.): SUNRISE 2023, CCIS 1884, pp. 71–89, 2024.
https://doi.org/10.1007/978-3-031-55829-0_5

1 Introduction

Integrating data analytics, digital transformation, and cybersecurity has become essential in the ever-changing healthcare landscape to ensure treatment efficiency, improve patient outcomes, and protect sensitive data. The convergence of technologies is transforming healthcare organizations and bringing previously unheard-of opportunities and challenges [1]. Through the ability to use enormous volumes of data to extract insightful information, improve decision-making procedures, and optimize operations, data analytics has become a disruptive force in healthcare organizations. Every day, healthcare organizations generate huge amounts of data, including operational data, medical imaging data, and patient records [2]. Healthcare providers can recognize patterns, forecast results, and customize patient care using advanced analytics [3].

Predictive analytics help medical practitioners anticipate health patterns, allocate resources optimally, and predict possible outbreaks. Prescriptive analytics also helps to create customized treatment programs based on past data and unique patient features [4]. These applications help optimize resources, reduce costs, and provide better patient care [5]. The healthcare sector is experiencing a significant change due to potential advancements in digital healthcare. Integrating digital technologies is completely transforming the provision, accessibility, and management of healthcare services [6]. Electronic Health Records have become essential to contemporary healthcare because they allow efficient information sharing between providers, streamline documentation, and increase productivity [7]. Telemedicine has grown exponentially since significant world events like the Covid-19 pandemic, which made remote healthcare delivery necessary. Patients can monitor long-term ailments, obtain prescriptions, and consult with doctors from the security of their homes. The increased use of wearable technology and the Internet of Things (IoTs) in healthcare organizations makes real-time patient monitoring possible. It enables proactive interventions and individualized treatment plans [8].

As healthcare transitions to the usage of digital technology, strong cybersecurity measures are essential. Cyber-attacks target healthcare organizations mainly because of the valuable and sensitive patient data stored in electronic systems. Cyber-attacks can lead to identity theft, compromising patients' privacy and disrupting essential healthcare services [9]. Robust cybersecurity frameworks should be implemented to protect patients' information and maintain healthcare systems' reliability. This involves implementing access controls to prevent unauthorized access, encrypting critical data, and safeguarding network infrastructures. Healthcare personnel must receive regular training on cybersecurity best practices to mitigate human-related risks such as phishing attacks [10]. This study focuses on the increasing concerns related to data security in digital health systems used by healthcare organizations. This study examines the relationship between cybersecurity investments and interdependence, uncertainty, knowledge, and security in digital transformation. The findings aid policymakers in developing healthcare to be more digitally resilient. The significant contributions to this study are as follows:

- To analyze the connections between Knowledge (KW), Uncertainty (UC), Interdependence (ID), and Security in digital transformation (SIT) of healthcare organizations, which improves understanding of the digital transformation process.
- To design an effective data-gathering method with Likert scale responses from healthcare organization managers as respondents.
- To propose a conceptual framework, six hypotheses undergo validation. This study delves into correlations centered around ID, UC, and cybersecurity KW.

The results of this research offer valuable insights for healthcare professionals and policymakers, providing information that can enhance digital resilience within healthcare organizations and effectively address data security concerns.

The remainder of this paper is structured as follows. Section 2 discusses related works. The development of the hypotheses and relevant methods are illustrated in Sect. 3. The results are explained in Sect. 4, followed by a discussion in Sect. 5. Finally, our conclusions and future work directions are provided in Sect. 6.

2 Related Works

Pramanik et al. [11] explored big data in healthcare analytics and informatics. They focused on the convergence of these domains, underscoring their importance in improving healthcare systems. They offered insightful viewpoints on utilizing big data for better decision-making and efficiency in healthcare settings as they addressed important discoveries and applications. Syed et al. [12] presented an intelligent healthcare framework for ambient assisted living using the Internet of Medical Things (IoMT) and big data analytics. They focused on improving healthcare through intelligent observation and evaluation of information gathered from diverse sources—the proposed framework aimed to enhance the standard of care and facilitate prompt interventions. Awad et al. [13] presented a study on the transformative effect of digital health technologies on patient care. The integration of interlinked healthcare systems was safeguarded, underscoring their potential to enhance healthcare delivery. The authors emphasized technologies' contribution to improving patient treatment outcomes and encouraging effective medical procedures. Nguyen et al. [14] proposed a study using a Deep Belief Network with the ResNet framework to integrate secured blockchain technologies into healthcare Cyber-Physical Systems (CPS). This framework improved healthcare data security in CPS by utilizing the resilience of blockchain and deep neural networks. This framework mainly protects sensitive information in healthcare settings.

Brown et al. [15] studied the factors influencing healthcare professionals' cybersecurity-related IoMT protective behaviors. They explored the factors that impact IoMT security protocols in healthcare organizations and offered significant perspectives for improving cybersecurity protocols. Pirbhulal et al. [16] proposed a framework integrating medical data security and resource efficiency for wearable healthcare systems. This framework focused on achieving an optimal balance between maximizing resource utilization and ensuring the security of sensitive medical information. This suggested method advances the general safety and functionality of wearable medical technology.

Karunarathne et al. [17] analyzed the confidentiality and security problems in IoT-based healthcare systems. They focused on the connection between the IoT and healthcare, addressed the difficulties, and suggested approaches to protect confidential health data. They emphasized the importance of strong security measures to protect healthcare data in IoT environments. Agrawal et al. [18] studied the security threats associated with web applications for healthcare. They evaluated the security of these applications and highlighted insights into potential vulnerabilities utilizing a fuzzy-based hybrid technique for multi-criteria decision-making analysis. This study improved the comprehension of security problems in healthcare web applications. Zhang et al. [19] focused on utilizing homomorphic encryption-based security-preserving federated learning to improve security in IoT-enabled healthcare systems. They examined the secure decentralized device collaboration to encrypt sensitive data during learning. This method addressed privacy issues with sharing healthcare data in IoT. Singh et al. [20] provided a mobile-edge computing framework for secure smart healthcare that uses chaotic and lightweight DNA sequences. This method ensured privacy and integrity while improving data security in smart healthcare systems. The fusion of chaos and DNA sequences offered an adequate basis for secure interaction in the IoT. Zhou et al. [21] presented a logistic regression-based privacy-preserving diagnostic method for digital healthcare. They provided an approach that ensured the privacy of patient data during the diagnostic process. Their approach, which employed logistic regression to provide precise diagnoses in digital healthcare systems, improves patient privacy. They focused on secure and efficient healthcare data analysis, which can increase patient privacy and diagnosis precision.

This study aims to analyze these limitations, enhancing data analytics, digital transformation, and safeguarding sensitive healthcare data in a connected world. This study also enhances the field by conducting a comprehensive analysis of the relationship between KW, UC, ID, and SIT of healthcare organizations. It also provides practical insights to enhance digital resilience and address concerns related to data security.

3 Hypotheses Development and Conceptual Framework

Figure 1 depicts the study's conceptual framework, such as the primary independent variables labeled UC and ID. The dependent variables are KW and SIT, which are formed by the interaction of these components. The following four primary constructs are used in this study:

- **KW:** This is measured using indicators KW1, KW2, and KW3, which measure the depth of comprehension of the information.
- **UC:** This is measured using indicators UC1, UC2, and UC3 to determine the unpredictable or unclear situation.
- **ID:** This is determined using indicators ID1, ID2, and ID3 to determine the interconnected elements.
- **SIT:** This is measured using indicators SIT1, SIT2, and SIT3 to determine the effectiveness of security measures during transformative processes.

These constructs and the indicators' parameters correspond to essential components of the study's analysis and help provide a deeper understanding of healthcare organizations. The six formulated hypotheses are as follows:

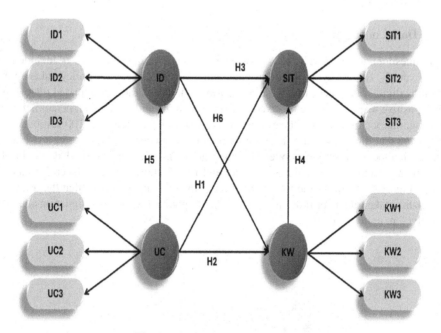

Fig. 1. The Conceptual Framework

- **H1 (Hypothesis 1):** There is a positive correlation between the organization's comprehension of the uncertainty (UC) in the digital domain and the security of its digital transformation (SIT) potential. (UC → SIT)
- **H2 (Hypothesis 2):** There is a positive relationship between the organization's comprehension of uncertainty (UC) in the digital age, its knowledge (KW) of the cybersecurity problem, and its economic investments in cybersecurity solutions. (UC → KW)
- **H3 (Hypotheses 3):** There is a positive correlation across the organization's comprehension of the interdependence (ID) between the digital resilience of its process and its level of security in its digital transformation (SIT). (ID → SIT)
- **H4 (Hypothesis 4):** There is a positive correlation between an organization's knowledge (KW) of cybersecurity issues, financial commitment to cybersecurity solutions, and the security of its digital transformative (SIT) potential. (KW → SIT)
- **H5 (Hypothesis 5):** There is a positive connection between the organization's ability to understand uncertainty (UC) in the digital space and recognition of the interdependence (ID) between digital and cyber resilience. (UC → ID)

- **H6 (Hypothesis 6):** There is a positive connection between the organization's comprehension of the interdependence (ID) between its digital strength, process, knowledge (KW) of the cybersecurity challenge, and its investments in cybersecurity solutions. (ID → KW)

3.1 Data Collection

The questionnaire is developed to collect the data. The questionnaire is included in Annexure 1. This study aimed to provide valuable perspectives for policymakers concerning digital resilience and digital transformation. Out of the 250 intended recipients, 100 positive responses were received through telephone and email from personnel with managerial positions in healthcare-related organizations. Among the 100 respondents, 55 stated that their companies allocate funds for cybersecurity, while 35 reported lacking such allocation. The respondents' demographic information is provided in Table 1. Figure 2 presents the organization's size, and Fig. 3 shows the cybersecurity budget ratio. Figure 4 illustrates the job distribution of the respondents. Note that the usage of the name stakeholder for those managers who do not have specific designations but are involved in management.

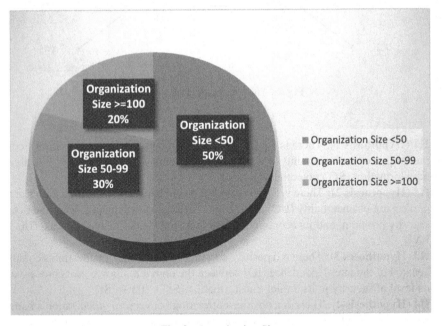

Fig. 2. Organization Size

The 100 responses from healthcare organization personnel are analyzed together to reduce bias by concentrating on SIT, KW, UC, and ID. The independent sample t-test showed no significant changes in the two groups ($p = 0.493, p = 0.272, p = 0.225$ and $p = 0.790$, respectively). This study addressed non-response bias and

Table 1. Demographic Characteristics of Respondents'

Demographics (N = 100)		Percentage (%)
Organization Size	Organization Size (<50)	50%
	Organization Size (50 – 99)	30%
	Organization Size (>= 100)	20%
Budget Allocation for Cybersecurity	Don't Know	10%
	No	35%
	Yes	55%
Job Role	Stakeholder	7%
	Chief Executive Officer (CEO)/General Manager (GM)/President/Chairperson	5%
	Chief Financial Officer (CFO)/Director of Finance	1%
	Chief Operating Officer (COO)	20%
	Chief Information Officer (CIO)	5%
	Chief Knowledge Officer (CKO)	10%
	Other Chief Officer or Managerial Position	7%
	Senior Vice President/Executive	1%
	Director of Management	1%
	Department Head	35%
	Director of the Department	7%
	Sub/Deupty Director	1%

employed Harman's factor single factor test to reduce data bias. Post-hoc analysis showed a significant common technique bias, with the unrelated factor solution explaining only 41.22% of the variation. Furthermore, a confirmatory factor analysis of Harman's test confirmed the absence of significant common technique bias, which showed a superior match for the measurement framework than the one-factor framework.

3.2 Research Instruments

A research tool has been created to analyze the data collection on data analytics, digital transformation, and cybersecurity perspectives in healthcare. Developing a questionnaire with five primary elements is the initial step in this procedure.

Demographic Information: This section comprised three questions designed to learn more about the respondents.

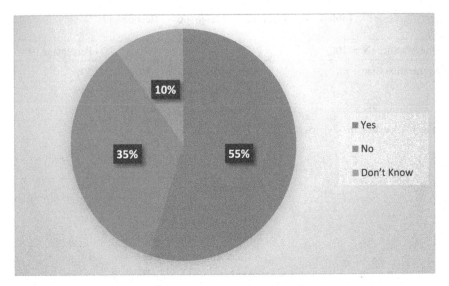

Fig. 3. Cybersecurity Budget Ratio

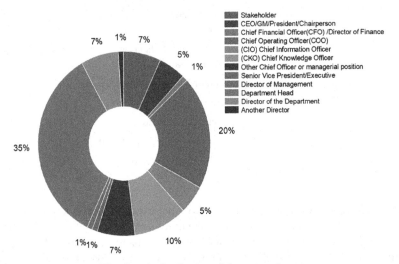

Fig. 4. Job distribution of the respondents

KW: This section consisted of three questions importance of cybersecurity knowledge and resource allocation.

UC: This section consisted of three questions that examined the effectiveness of prevention measures and component interactions to assess the digital uncertainty of the organization.

ID: This section consisted of three questions that assessed its digital resilience and process of interdependence.

SIT: The final section included three questions that evaluated digital transformation using cybersecurity, data protection, and communication elements.

The customized form had five essential parts, and answers were asked to be given on a Likert scale of 5 points, rated (1) "completely disagree" to (5) "completely agree".

3.3 Statistical Analysis

This study analyzed data with SmartPLS 29.0. This study tests hypotheses within a framework to maximize the dependent variable's explained variance while considering performance indices. The framework is evaluated in two steps: measurement framework and structural framework. Each composite's indicators' path coefficients (PC), fit indices, weights, and loadings were bootstrapped to calculate significance to address variation difficulties. Since the Partial Least Squares Structural Equation Modeling (PLS-SEM) analysis confirmed the structural framework, fit values were measured for the saturation framework based on the proposed framework.

4 Results

4.1 Framework Measurements

Fit indices used in Structural Equation Modeling (SEM) to evaluate the quality of the framework of fit are the Standardized Root Mean Square Residual (SRMR), Unweighted Least Squares Discrepancy (d_{ULS})

(, and Geodesic Discrepancy (d_G)

The description of every of these fit indices as follows:

Standardized Root Mean Square Residual (SRMR): The mean absolute standardized residual is measured using the SRMR parameter. The square root of the average of squared variations between the actual and predicted covariance is computed, standardizing the result by the calculated residual covariance matrix and using Eq. (1) to calculate SRMR.

$$\text{SRMR} = \sqrt{\frac{\sum_{i,j}(\widehat{\sigma}_{ij} - \sigma_{ij})^2}{\sum_{i,j}\widehat{\sigma}_{ij}^2 + \sum_{i,j}\sigma_{ij}^2}} \tag{1}$$

where $\widehat{\sigma}_{ij}$ represents the estimated correlation between variables *i and j*, and σ_{ij} denotes the measured covariance between variables *i and j*.

Unweighted Least Squares Discrepancy (d_{ULS}):

The difference between the sample covariance matrix and the covariance matrix that the framework implies is measured by (d_{ULS}).

The unweighted least squares discrepancy is calculated using Eq. (2).

$$d_{ULS} = \sqrt{\sum_{i,j} \left(\frac{S_{ij} - \hat{S}_{ij}}{1 + \hat{S}_{ij}} \right)^2} \qquad (2)$$

Geodesic Discrepancy(d_G): An additional metric for measuring the difference between a covariance matrix predicted by the framework and the sample covariance matrix is (d_G)

The geodesic discrepancy is calculated using Eq. (3).

$$d_G = \sqrt{\sum_{i,j} \left(\frac{S_{ij} - \hat{S}_{ij}}{1 - \hat{S}_{ij}} \right)^2} \qquad (3)$$

where S_{ij} represents the sample correlation between variables i and j, and $\hat{S}_{ij}$ represents the correlation between variables i and j as indicated by the framework.

The results demonstrated in Table 2 indicate that every fit index for the saturated framework meets the requirements needed to validate the suggested measurement framework. The framework's fit statistics using Partial Least Squares (PLS) show that it fits satisfactorily, with anSRMR with a value of 0.077. In addition, every discrepancy is below the bootstrap discrepancies' 99%-quantile (Hi99), suggesting a perfect fit for the measurement framework. This implies that the conceptual framework and reality matrix are strongly aligned. PLS-SEM analyzes the path coefficients' sign, magnitudes, significance, and essential structural framework outcomes. The determination coefficient (R^2), which represents the clarified variation of dependent variables, is the objective of the PLS-SEM algorithm. The impact size f^2, which illustrates how the R^2 changes when a particular construct is removed from the framework. Small, medium, and significant effects are represented by standards of $0.03, 0.16$, and 0.36, respectively. This study used a non-parametric test using percentile confidence intervals and parametric tests like t-values, as shown in Table 3. Additionally, the 95% Confidence Interval (CI) of the bootstrapped standardized direct effect does not include zero, indicating the importance of the direct impact.

Table 2. Comparison of Estimated Frameworks (Hi95, Hi99)

Framework	Saturated	Hi95	Hi99	Estimated	Hi95	Hi99
SRMR	0.073	0.076	0.083	0.073	0.077	0.090
d_G	0.219	0.265	0.332	0.219	0.262	0.299
d_{ULS}	0.397	0.424	0.509	0.397	0.446	0.608

Table 3. Structural Framewor

ypothesis	PC	5%CI$_{low}$	95%CI$_{high}$	Significance ($p-value$)	Cohen's f^2	R^2
H1: UC → SIT	0.293	0.032	0.552	0.032	0.134	0.542
H2: UC → KW	0.372	0.152	0.597	0.003	0.103	0.354
H3: ID → SIT	0.345	0.077	0.670	0.028	0.178	0.542
H4: KW → SIT	0.286	0.061	0.496	0.013	0.161	0.542
H5: UC → ID	0.396	0.141	0.672	0.006	0.195	0.157
H6: ID → KW	0.343	0.132	0.554	0.003	0.094	0.354

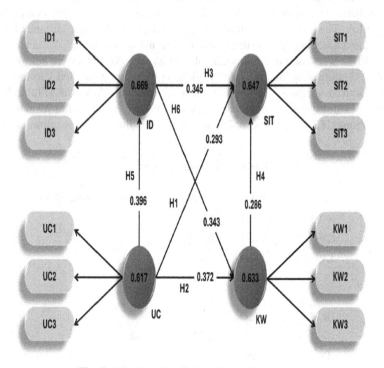

Fig. 5. The Path Coefficient for the Hypotheses

Figure 5 depicts the path coefficient for the hypotheses. The findings of a hypothesis test investigating the connections among KW, SIT, UC, and ID in healthcare organizations. The PC indicates the direction and strength of these relationships. Significantly, uncertainty positively impacts knowledge (H2: UC → KW) and digital transformation (H1: UC → SIT), indicating that when uncertainty increases, so does the importance of knowledge acquisition and digital transformation. Additionally, interdependence positively impacts knowledge (H6: ID → KW) and digital transformation (H3: ID → SIT), emphasizing its role in determining both. Knowledge has a positive effect on digital transformation (H4: KW → SIT). The relationships' validity is supported by the path coefficients, which have p-values less than 0.05 and are statistically significant. The R^2 value for each hypothesis indicates that the suggested frameworks explain significant variance in the corresponding dependent variables, and Cohen's f^2 values show moderate effect sizes. The findings provide insightful information about the intricate dynamics of digital transformation in healthcare organizations.

4.2 Structural Framework

The measurement framework was evaluated using a PLS-SEM, and the results show that it meets generally recognized reliability and validity standards. Firstly, every construct's standardized loading exceeds the threshold of 0.70, confirming individual reliability. Furthermore, combined reliability metrics exceed 0.80, signifying comprehensive dependability. The convergent validity is approved by the Average Variance Extracted (AVE) values exceeding the 0.50 threshold, as demonstrated in Table 4. Variance Inflation Factors (VIFs) were used in a thorough collinearity test. All VIFs were below a critical value of 3.33, suggesting that the framework had no Common-Method Variance (CMV) problems with a maximum VIF of 2.098, there are minimal CMV issues (Table 5). Also, discriminant validity is demonstrated since each construct's Heterotrait-Monotrait Ratio of Correlations (HTMT) values are less than 0.90. The findings of discriminant validity

Table 4. Assessment Framework

Constructs	Indicator	VIFs	Loadings	Combined Reliability	AVE
KW	KW1	1.423	0.734	0.838	0.633
	KW 2	1.657	0.871		
	KW 13	1.309	0.776		
UC	UC1	1.438	0.824	0.829	0.617
	UC 2	1.359	0.791		
	UC 3	1.256	0.741		
ID	ID1	1.823	0.836	0.859	0.669
	ID2	1.299	0.723		
	ID3	2.098	0.889		
SIT	SIT1	1.515	0.823	0.847	0.647
	SIT2	1.429	0.819		
	SIT3	1.369	0.771		

are further supported by the reality that each construct shows a more significant correlation with its measure of validity than with other measures. Figure 6 illustrates the
graphical representation of the measurement framework.

Table 5. Discriminant Validity

Construct	UC	SIT	KW	ID
UC	**0.785**	0.802	0.737	0.555
SIT	0.571	**0.803**	0.821	0.816
KW	0.506	0.599	**0.795**	0.648
ID	0.396	0.598	0.488	**0.818**

UC → UC; ID → ID; KW → KW; SIT → SIT. Diagonal values (square root of
AVE are in bold). HTMT thresholds are shown above the diagonal line.

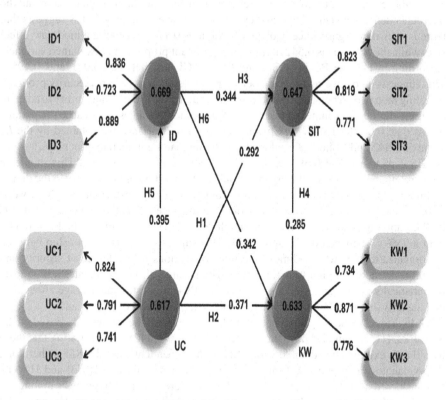

Fig. 6. Graphical Representation of the Measurement Framework's Evaluation

5 Discussion

In H1, the PC is 0.293, and the 5% CI ranges between 0.032 and 0. and 0.552. s suggests a strong correlation between the organization's investments in cybersecurity solutions and its comprehension of the interdependence of digital strength, procedure, and cybersecurity knowledge. This relationship may be statistically significant because the significance level (p-value) is 0.032, less than the standard cutoff of 0.05. With an R^2 value of 0.542 and a Cohen's f^2 value of 0.134, which suggests a moderate effect size, the framework can explain significant variation in the dependent variable. In H2, the PC is 0.372, with a 95% CI ranging from 0.15 to 0.597. This suggests a favorable correlation between comprehension of uncertainty in the digital era, expertise in cybersecurity, and financial investments in cybersecurity solutions. The p-value is 0.003, indicating statistical significance as it is below the threshold of 0.05. The Cohen's f^2 value is 0.103, indicating a moderate effect size. Additionally, the R^2 value is 0.354 indicating that the framework explains a significant proportion of the variability in the dependent variable.

H3 shows a PC of 0.345, with a 95% CI ranging from 0.07 to 0.670. This implies a favorable correlation between comprehending uncertainty in the digital realm and the interdependence between digital and cybersecurity. The p-value of 0.028 suggests that there is statistical significance. Cohen's f^2 value is 0.178, indicating a moderate effect size, while the R^2 value is 0.542, marking a significant proportion of explained variance. According to H4, the PC is 0.286, and the 5% CI falls between 0.061 and 0.496. . This suggests a positive relationship between understanding the cybersecurity problem, investing money in cybersecurity solutions, and having the security and ability to adapt to changing digital environments. Statistical significance is suggested because the p-value is less than 0.05 (0.013). A significant amount of the variance is explained by the R^2 value of 0.542 and Cohen's f^2 value of 00.161 indicates a moderate effect size.

H5 depicts a PC of 0.396, with a 5% CI between 0.141 to 0.672 This implies a direct relationship between the organization's understanding of uncertainty in the digital realm and the level of security in its potential for digital transformation. The p-value of 0.006 indicates a high level of statistical significance. Cohen's--squared f^2 value is 0.195, implying an average effect size and the R^2 value is 0.157. In H6, the PC is 0.343, with a 95% CI between 0.132 and 0.554. This suggests a direct relationship between the organization's understanding of the interconnections in the degree of security and digital resilience in digital transformation. The p-value of 0.003 indicates a high level of statistical significance. Cohen's f^2 value is 0.094, suggesting an average effect size, and the R^2 value is 0.354, describing a significant proportion of the variance.

A higher R^2 value suggests a better predictive power of the framework. Based on the R^2 values, H1, H3, and H4 have the greatest R^2 values (0.542), demonstrating that these hypotheses explain considerable variability in the dependent variable (SIT). Therefore, the explanatory power of the framework in terms of R^2 values, H1, H3, and H4, can be considered as the best hypothesis, can be considered the best hypothesis among the other hypotheses. The results demonstrate that three important factors directly affect the security layer of healthcare organizations' digital transformational capabilities, as illustrated by H1, H3, and H4.

6 Conclusions

This study discusses increasing concerns about data security in the healthcare organization. Findings show a strong positive relation between the healthcare organization's understanding of ID, UC, KW, SIT, and cybersecurity solution investments. Policymakers can use the study's results to inform and guide policy decisions related to data security in healthcare organizations. The results demonstrate a positive relationship between cybersecurity knowledge, interdependence understanding, and acquisitions in cybersecurity solutions through statistical validation using SmartPLS. Policymakers can use this information to emphasize the need for healthcare organizations to enhance their understanding of these components, leading to more informed policy directions. This analysis shows that hypotheses H1, H3, and H4 significantly impact digital transformation security layers, with the greatest values (0.542), offering policymakers important information for improving digital resilience. Policymakers can use the insights from the study to optimize investments in cybersecurity solutions. Acknowledging that healthcare industries face privacy issues, policymakers can focus on developing policie between data security and privacy. This could involve the creation of regulations and guidelines that ensure robust cybersecurity measures without compromising patient privacy.

Policymakers can use the study's findings to guide future research directions. The inclusion of AI integration and cybersecurity as identified areas for future studies indicates potential for policymakers to support research initiatives that delve deeper into these aspects, contributing to ongoing efforts to improve digital resilience in healthcare.

Annexure 1

Section 1: Demographic Information
Organization Size:

- Organization Size (<50)
- Organization Size ($50 - 99$)
- Organization Size ($> = 100$)

   A Financial Allocation for Cybersecurity:

- Don't Know
- No
- Yes

   Job Role:

- Stakeholder
- Chief Executive Officer (CEO)/General Manager (GM)/President/Chairperson
- Chief Financial Officer (CFO)/Director of Finance
- Chief Operating Officer (COO)
- Chief Information Officer (CIO)
- Chief Knowledge Officer (CKO)
- Other Chief Officer or Managerial Position
- Senior Vice President/Executive
- Director of Management

- Department Head
- Director of the Department
- Another Director

(Instructions: Please rate your agreement with the following statements regarding your healthcare organization in 4.0.)

Questionnaire 1: Knowledge (KW)

1. Our management board is sufficiently aware of the risks that digital technologies present to our company at this time.

   - Strongly Disagree
   - Disagree
   - Neutral
   - Agree
   - Strongly Agree

2. Effective procedures are in place at our organization for identifying, reducing, and handling cybersecurity incidents.

   - Strongly Disagree
   - Disagree
   - Neutral
   - Agree
   - Strongly Agree

3. Our organization periodically assesses how much cybersecurity is integrated into our daily operations.

   - Strongly Disagree
   - Disagree
   - Neutral
   - Agree
   - Strongly Agree

Questionnaire 2: Uncertainty (UC)

1. Our organization is sufficiently aware of the interdependencies between the main digital assets and services.

   - Strongly Disagree
   - Disagree
   - Neutral
   - Agree
   - Strongly Agree

2. If we lose access to a vital digital asset (like a specific database or application), our organization is equipped with efficient procedures to continue operating.

- Strongly Disagree
- Disagree
- Neutral
- Agree
- Strongly Agree

3. Our organization's cybersecurity risk has increased due to the ongoing COVID-19 crisis.

- Strongly Disagree
- Disagree
- Neutral
- Agree
- Strongly Agree

Questionnaire 3: Interdependence (ID)

1. Our organization is a part of an external partnership or program that exchanges cybersecurity knowledge and expertise.

- Strongly Disagree
- Disagree
- Neutral
- Agree
- Strongly Agree

2. Our organization is confident in the cybersecurity protocols that our suppliers, vendors, and service providers have implemented.

- Strongly Disagree
- Disagree
- Neutral
- Agree
- Strongly Agree

3. Our organization routinely examines our supply chain's adherence to cyber security regulations.

- Strongly Disagree
- Disagree
- Neutral
- Agree
- Strongly Agree

Questionnaire 4: Security in Transformation (SIT)

1. Our organization has effective protocols for external communication in the event of a cybersecurity incident.

- Strongly Disagree
- Disagree
- Neutral
- Agree
- Strongly Agree

2. Our organization has a solid plan to protect our data.

- Strongly Disagree
- Disagree
- Neutral
- Agree
- Strongly Agree

3. Our management board frequently participates in cyber wargames and tabletop exercises.

- Strongly Disagree
- Disagree
- Neutral
- Agree
- Strongly Agree

References

1. Möller, D.P.: Cybersecurity in digital transformation. In: Guide to Cybersecurity in Digital Transformation: Trends, Methods, Technologies, Applications and Best Practices, pp. 1–70. Springer, Cham (2023). https://doi.org/10.1007/978-3-031-26845-8_1
2. Azzaoui, A.E., Sharma, P.K., Park, J.H.: Blockchain-based delegated quantum cloud architecture for medical big data security. J. Netw. Comput. Appl. **198**, 103304 (2022)
3. Kumar, P., Kumar, R., Gupta, G.P., Tripathi, R., Jolfaei, A., Islam, A.N.: A blockchain-orchestrated deep learning approach for secure data transmission in IoT-enabled healthcare systems. J. Parallel Distrib. Comput. **172**, 69–83 (2023)
4. Batko, K., Ślęzak, A.: The use of big data analytics in healthcare. J. Big Data **9**(1), 3 (2022)
5. Hayyolalam, V., Aloqaily, M., Özkasap, Ö., Guizani, M.: Edge intelligence for empowering IoT-based healthcare systems. IEEE Wirel. Commun. **28**(3), 6–14 (2021)
6. Aminizadeh, S., et al.: The applications of machine learning techniques in medical data processing based on distributed computing and the internet of things. Comput. Methods Program. Biomedicine **241**, 107745 (2023)
7. Mohammed-Nasir, R., Oshikoya, K.A., Oreagba, I.A.: Digital innovation in healthcare entrepreneurship. In: Raimi, L., Oreagba, I.A. (eds.) Medical Entrepreneurship, pp. 341–372. Springer, Singapore (2023). https://doi.org/10.1007/978-981-19-6696-5_22
8. Trenfield, S.J., et al.: Advancing pharmacy and healthcare with virtual digital technologies. Adv. Drug Deliv. Rev. **182**, 114098 (2022)
9. Ambarkar, S.S., Shekokar, N.: Toward smart and secure IoT based healthcare system. In: Dey, N., Mahalle, P., Shafi, P., Kimabahune, V., Hassanien, A. (eds.) Internet of Things, Smart Computing and Technology: A Roadmap Ahead. Studies in Systems, Decision and Control, vol. 266, pp. 283–303. Springer, Cham (2020). https://doi.org/10.1007/978-3-030-39047-1_13

10. Chenthara, S., Ahmed, K., Wang, H., Whittaker, F.: Security and privacy-preserving challenges of e-health solutions in cloud computing. IEEE Access **7**, 74361–74382 (2019)
11. Pramanik, M.I., Lau, R.Y., Azad, M.A.K., Hossain, M.S., Chowdhury, M.K.H., Karmaker, B.K.: Healthcare informatics and analytics in big data. Expert Syst. Appl. **152**, 113388 (2020)
12. Syed, L., Jabeen, S., Manimala, S., Alsaeedi, A.: Smart healthcare framework for ambient assisted living using IoMT and big data analytics techniques. Futur. Gener. Comput. Syst. **101**, 136–151 (2019)
13. Awad, A., et al.: Connected healthcare: improving patient care using digital health technologies. Adv. Drug Deliv. Rev. **178**, 113958 (2021)
14. Nguyen, G.N., Le Viet, N.H., Elhoseny, M., Shankar, K., Gupta, B.B., Abd El-Latif, A.A.: Secure Blockchain enabled cyber-physical systems in healthcare using deep belief network with ResNet framework. J. Parallel Distrib. Comput. **153**, 150–160 (2021)
15. Brown, S., Ruhwanya, Z., Pekane, A.: Factors influencing internet of medical things (IoMT) cybersecurity protective behaviours among healthcare workers. In: Furnell, S., Clarke, N. (eds.) Human Aspects of Information Security and Assurance. HAISA 2023. IFIP Advances in Information and Communication Technology, vol. 674, pp. 432–444. Springer, Cham (2023). https://doi.org/10.1007/978-3-031-38530-8_34
16. Pirbhulal, S., Samuel, O.W., Wu, W., Sangaiah, A.K., Li, G.: A joint resource-aware and medical data security framework for wearable healthcare systems. Futur. Gener. Comput. Syst. **95**, 382–391 (2019)
17. Karunarathne, S.M., Saxena, N., Khan, M.K.: Security and privacy in IoT smart healthcare. IEEE Internet Comput. **25**(4), 37–48 (2021)
18. Agrawal, A., et al.: Evaluating the security impact of healthcare web applications through fuzzy based hybrid approach of multi-criteria decision-making analysis. IEEE Access **8**, 135770–135783 (2020)
19. Zhang, L., Xu, J., Vijayakumar, P., Sharma, P.K., Ghosh, U.: Homomorphic encryption-based privacy-preserving federated learning in IoT-enabled healthcare system. IEEE Trans. Network Sci. Eng. **10**, 2864–2880 (2022)
20. Singh, A., Chatterjee, K., Singh, A.K., Kumar, N.: Secure smart healthcare framework using lightweight DNA sequence and chaos for mobile-edge computing. IEEE Internet Things J. **10**(6), 4883–4890 (2022)
21. Zhou, Y., et al.: A privacy-preserving logistic regression-based diagnosis scheme for digital healthcare. Futur. Gener. Comput. Syst. Comput. Syst. **144**, 63–73 (2023)

Methodology for Automating Attacking Agents in Cyber Range Training Platforms

Pablo Martínez Sánchez[1] ⓘ, Pantaleone Nespoli[1,2(✉)] ⓘ, Joaquín García Alfaro[2] ⓘ, and Félix Gómez Mármol[1] ⓘ

[1] Department of Information and Communications Engineering, University of Murcia, 30100 Murcia, Spain
{pablo.martinezs2,pantaleone.nespoli,felixgm}@um.es
[2] SAMOVAR, Télécom SudParis, Institut Polytechnique de Paris, 19 place Marguerite Perey, 91120 Palaiseau, France
{pantaleone.nespoli,joaquin.garcia_alfaro}@telecom-sudparis.eu

Abstract. The world faces cyberattacks daily and the targets of these attacks are often critical infrastructure, including the healthcare sector. In addition, more than half of cybersecurity professionals lack the necessary knowledge to deploy the relevant countermeasures to these attacks. In this regard, there is no doubt that education and training in cybersecurity are essential to defend technological assets. That is why, in this context, it is easy to understand that Cyber Ranges play a crucial role since these tools provide the user with a hyper-realistic experience for quality training. Thanks to attack simulators, commonly Advanced Persistent Threats (APT) generators, those realistic defensive cyberexercises can be performed. To implement these components, a behavioral matrix is needed, marking the different stages used by a cybersecurity expert during an attack, e.g. reconnaissance, explotation, data exfiltration, etc. Since bringing the current methodologies to a hyper-realistic production environment is an inordinate challenge, a novel matrix will be designed from simulation environments for training. This new methodology will compact dependent phases and simplify similar stages to automatically. Furthermore, the contribution contains a logic that increases the reality of the attacks. Finally, a proof of concept is made to evaluate the purposes the contribution purses.

Keywords: Attack methodology · Advanced Persistent Threat · Cyber Range · Cybersecurity · Critical Infrastructure

1 Introduction

Investment in cybersecurity increases every year despite not seeing a robust result against cyberattacks since, as studies published by CSIS (Center for Strategic and International Studies) state, this investment in security and research is still not sufficient [1]. Specifically, in the previous report, one can observe the evolution of the United States and China in this field, attributed to their investment to innovation and self-reliance, independent of other powers.

The healthcare sector, a critical pillar of modern society, is alarmingly vulnerable regarding cybersecurity [2]. This vulnerability is not just a theoretical concern; it has

H. Abie et al. (Eds.): SUNRISE 2023, CCIS 1884, pp. 90–109, 2024.
https://doi.org/10.1007/978-3-031-55829-0_6

been well-documented and widely acknowledged by industry experts and professionals, as reported in [3,4]. The complex network of interconnected devices, medical records, and patient data forms a repository of sensitive information that is highly attractive for potential exploitation because this software often does not count with continuous updates, like Internet of Things (IoT) devices [5]. Cyber terrorists, recognizing this weakness, frequently target healthcare institutions, not just for the valuable data they hold but also to exploit the life-saving nature of these institutions. A successful cyberattack can disrupt medical services, putting countless lives at risk [6]. As such, there is an urgent need for the healthcare sector to bolster its defenses and prioritize cybersecurity, ensuring the safety and well-being of its patients.

To study the impact of attacks suffered, techniques have been used to quantify the different security postures of networks by simulating cyberattacks. Some of these tests are i) Traditional Explotation tests, which focus on testing the robustness, security, and integrity of the network, and ii) Red Team exercises, where a group of experts simulate a realistic attack where they try to compromise the network by imitating the attacks carried out by cybercriminals [7]. As it can be seen, both are carried out by teams of people, which means that these tests: i) are not completely reliable, given the human error rate caused by, for example, fatigue, and ii) are costly, due to the large outlay involved in hiring an experienced professional. For this reason, the great challenge of automating the actions performed by experts and cybercriminals is born. In particular, the main objective is to achieve: i) robustness, to ensure determinism; ii) scalability, to be able to replicate the tests as many times as necessary; iii) and low cost of the results, compared to a realistic simulation of an attack [8].

One of the most powerful and largely-used tools for training cybersecurity professionals is the Cyber Range platform, where gamification, team confrontations, etc. can be implemented. These platforms are virtualization environments designed to simulate or emulate hyper-realistic environments where activities can be carried out, such as defensive and evasive actions, explotation, data exfiltration, etc [9]. Thanks to this type of tool, nowadays, users of a Cyber Range can acquire highly demanded skills in cybersecurity. Furthermore, according to the World Economic Forum report [10], 62% of cybersecurity professionals do not yet have the necessary skills to be able to respond to a cyberattack [11], including defending against novel and disruptive attacks, such as zero-day attacks.

In this context, it is worth remarking that simulating a realistic attack from which the users of a Cyber Range must defend themselves and/or the simulated infrastructure is a highly complex challenge. These simulations are designed to imitate actual cyber threats and, therefore, require a deep understanding of current cybersecurity threats, tactics, and techniques. The complexity arises not only from the need to create a believable and relevant attack scenario but also from the necessity to adapt and evolve these scenarios in real-time in response to the actions and decisions of the trainees.

This dynamic interplay ensures that the Cyber Range provides an immersive and educational experience, pushing users to apply their knowledge and skills in a high-stakes, controlled environment. The ultimate goal is to prepare cybersecurity professionals for the unpredictable and ever-evolving nature of real-world cyber threats. Thus, the design and execution of these simulations represent a crucial tasks.

The intricacies of real-world scenarios make it a demanding task to replicate accurately. That is why the methodology employed for conducting the attack should be comprehensively and inclusively defined to enable its adaptation to scenarios not previously encountered by the tool. Despite the existence of attack methodologies that define this casuistry, they do not necessarily meet these requirements, given the passage of time and the increasing complexity of new attack vectors. Therefore, this paper aims to answer the following research questions:

1. Can APT simulators follow realistic attack matrices?
2. Are APT simulators sufficiently autonomous to perform an attack?
3. Can APT simulators be useful to Cyber Range users to improve their cybersecurity skills?

To solve these questions, a novel attack methodology has been proposed that compacts, automates, and intercommunicates the different phases presented in the existing attack methodologies. In this sense, such a matrix responds to the abovementioned question 1. The new attack matrix has been trialed using a proof of concept in a Cyber Range setting. This was made possible through a novel framework and various design patterns and application programming interfaces allowing the attack simulator to use any offensive tool and make decisions with an environment it gradually knows, answering the abovementioned question 2. The improvement in the authenticity and adaptability of the attacker will directly impact the defensive maneuvers of the users, which in turn will improve the skills needed to respond effectively to a cyberattack as an answer to question 3.

The structure of the article is as follows. Section 2 analyzes the existing literature on attack methodologies. Then, Sect. 3 proposes the developed methodology that solves the raised problems. Section 4 exposes a tool-independent architecture using design patterns. Next, Sect. 5 contains the tool's poof of concept based on the proposed architecture. Finally, Sect. 6 summarizes the conclusions of the research presented and shows possible future lines of research.

2 State of the Art

Despite the vast increment in cybersecurity investment, the problem of finding a realistic attack simulator remains unresolved [12]. Presently, prominent national enterprises maintain teams of cybersecurity experts engaged in Red Team exercises. Each team member specializes in specific attack domains such as web services, mail services, firewalls, and more. Given the complexity of today's attacks, these experts follow their methodology based on their personal experience. In turn, they use tools that automate mechanical and repetitive actions, saving time and increasing the reliability of attacks. Examples of such tools are Nmap, for device enumeration; Hashcat, for checking insecure passwords; Burpsuite, for automating actions on web interfaces; among others [12].

Nowadays, systems have more protection measures, which means an increase in the complexity of attacks and tools that automate the exploitation of vulnerabilities to infect a system in a controlled or malicious way. This is why defining a methodology that standardizes all attack techniques requires much knowledge and is highly complex. Over time, several attack matrices have appeared, although there are now globally recognized classifications, such as MITRE ATT&CK [13] or Cyber Kill Chain (CKC) [14].

Specifically, MITRE ATT&CK is a globally accessible knowledge base on tactics (i.e., thematic sets of techniques) and techniques (i.e., attack sets based on real-world observations). The MITRE ATT&CK knowledge base is a foundation for developing specific threat models and methodologies in the private sector, government, and the cybersecurity products and services community. The matrix is created from a theoretical point of view and brings together the most commonly used attacks in real environments. The repository par excellence, which contains the implementation of attacks organized under the MITRE ATT&CK hierarchy, is the Atomic Red Team[1]. In particular, the matrix comprises the phases described and its unique identifier, as described in Table 1.

Table 1. MITRE ATT&CK's phases

Phase	ID	Description
Reconnaissance	TA0043	Gathering information
Resource Development	TA0042	Creation of support resources
Initial Access	TA0001	Network information gathering
Execution	TA0002	Vulnerability exploitation
Persistence	TA0003	Establishing persistence
Privilege Escalation	TA0004	Obtaining administrator rights
Defense Evasion	TA0005	Maneuvers to avoid detection
Credential Access	TA0006	Theft of users and passwords
Discovery	TA0007	Discovery of the internal environment
Lateral Movement	TA0008	Moving around the internal environment
Collection	TA0009	Gathering information of interest
Command and Control	TA0011	Communicating with compromised systems to control them
Exfiltration	TA0010	Theft of information
Impact	TA0040	Manipulation, disruption, and destruction

On the other hand, the CKC model of cybersecurity explains the typical procedure cybercriminals follow to complete a successful cyberattack. Concretely, it is a framework developed by Lockheed Martin, derived from military attack models, and translated to the digital world to help teams understand, detect, and prevent persistent cyber threats. It is comprised of the phases reported in Table 2.

Apart from the previous theoretical methodologies, practical approaches, such as the one provided by the expert Carlos Polop, i.e., HackTricks [15], can also be found. This methodology has been developed based on extensive experience on offensive security. In conjunction with this, one can discover a comprehensive description of the implementation of each attack vector. In particular, he explains to the user the reasoning

---

[1] https://atomicredteam.io/.

Table 2. Cyber Kill Chain's phases

Phase	Description
Recognition	Collection of information from open sources
Preparation	Selection and exploitation of attack vectors
Distribution	Distribution of malicious payload across systems
Exploitation	Exploitation of distributed malware
Installation	Establishment of persistence
Command & Control	Communication with compromised computers
Actions on Objective	Monitoring and post-exploitation

behind each decision taken in the methodology and describes the concepts, steps to follow, or configurations required for the tools involved in cybersecurity [15]. It comprises the phases reported in Table 3.

Table 3. HackTricks's phases

Phase	Description
Physical Attacks	Physical attacks on equipment
Discovering	Discovery of access routes and equipment
Discovering internal	Capturing sensitive information once inside the network
Port scan	Search for vulnerable services on computers
Searching service version exploits	Search for known vulnerabilities in services
Pentesting Services - Automatic Tools	Exploitation of vulnerabilities with automatic tools
Pentesting Services - Brute-Forcing services	Exploitation using brute force attacks
Phishing	If the previous steps did not work, phishing
Getting Shell	Obtaining means for the execution of remote commands
Inside	Execution of remote actions on victim machines
Exfiltration	Extracting and inserting files on the victim
Privilege Escalation - Local Privesc	Obtaining privileges on the victim machine
Privilege Escalation - Domain Privesc	Obtaining privileges in the organization
POST - Looting	Obtaining critical or confidential data
POST - Persistence	Establishing persistence
Pivoting	Infecting other computers connected to the victim

The above matrices contain valuable knowledge that should be taken into account when it comes to describe the steps that an attacker would make in a realistic situation. The problem with them is that the knowledge is too segmented, causing the software to fall into very rigid and sequential implementations. Despite being able to catalog different attacks accurately, MITRE ATT&CK's fragmentation complicates implementation. While the database's methodology of storing attacks is generic, which is not inherently negative, applying these attacks to a specific use case becomes more complex, as they are not designed for any particular environment. On the other hand, CKC has no mechanism that allows flexibility between the different phases. The design of this matrix is simple, yet it is closely interconnected in a way that can result in repetitive, predictable, and identifiable attacks, ultimately making it challenging to attach tools. Finally, Hack-Trick was created to introduce and teach people about pentesting, making it the most practical option. Nevertheless, it has drawbacks, too. Specifically, it is focused on the educational environment and not on the automation of attacks, making it very difficult to develop a tool. Moreover, the tool would have, again, the same problem: it would not be flexible enough to implement in a Cyber Range environment.

As mentioned above, the existing matrices have an informative approach and are far from being able to carry out hyper-realistic implementations in a Cyber Range environment. This is because fragmenting the stages with so much detail increases the complexity of automating them. Solving fragmentation would lead to software solutions that would very accurately simulate the activities performed by a human attacker, answering the question 1 posed in the introduction.

3   Methodology

The challenge that this paper aims to solve is to develop a methodology that is generic and flexible enough to be able to automate all kinds of realistic attacks within a training platform (e.g., Cyber Range platforms) where cybersecurity capabilities can be developed while answering questions mentioned above.

3.1   Matrix

The methodologies analyzed above do not represent a good fit with Cyber Ranges environments for the reasons given above. Despite this, given that they contain mature, widely used, and recognized knowledge, we will later contrast what knowledge is contained in the novel methodology with MITRE ATT&CK Table 1, CKC Table 2 and HackTricks Table 3.

This matrix is created with the motivation of compacting the highly dependent phases. In addition, the possible coupling of tools used by attackers is considered. The phases resulting from the exhaustive study conducted are reported in Table 4.

Table 4. Phases of the proposed novel matrix and their description

Phase	Description
Discovery	Discovery of information, equipment, and vulnerabilities
Explotation	Exploitation of vulnerabilities
Inside	Exfiltration, infiltration, and information gathering
Pivoting	Provisioning and infection of other computers connected to the victim

The *Discovery* phase includes everything related to the discovery of organizational information: finger/footprint (data collection in the public domain), the discovery of equipment, services, and vulnerabilities in the organization, the relationship between services and Common Vulnerabilities and Exposures (CVE), etc.

Next, *Explotation* encompasses all types of vulnerability exploitation: exploitation of CVEs, brute force and Denial of Service (DoS) attacks and remote code execution, among others.

Once the control of the computer has been taken, the next phase is the *Inside*, where all the actions that will occur inside the victim machine are carried out: data exfiltration, persistence, privilege escalation, just to cite some examples.

Finally, in certain situations, it is necessary to establish communication channels for lateral movement between different machines. This phase is called *Pivoting*.

All phases are encompassed by reasoning that relates and manages the dependencies between the abovementioned phases. Certainly, it is thanks to *Logic*, which will be explained in Sect. 3.2. In the case of a Cyber Range instructor, a skilled professional responsible for guiding, monitoring, and managing cyberexercises within the platform, this role enables the configuration and adaptation of the different stages to simulate an attack effectively.

The formulation of the suggested matrix arises from observing that various stages transpire concurrently during a specific attack phase and the pronounced interdependence of certain elements. The main objective is the attacker simulation is to achieve a target. Generally, such a target can have various forms in a training environment, e.g., retrieve a configuration or file, gaining access to an equip, denying a service, or getting root privileges, among others. After capturing a target, several actions are executed, allowing them to occur within the same phase. Similarly, some phases have a tight connection to the prior stage, paving the way for integration. Consequently, even though compressing the phases might lead to a marginal rise in complexity, it does not result in information loss. On the contrary, this condensation can enhance the automation of implementations using this approach.

Once the different stages have been defined, the reliability and completeness of the proposed methodology must be supported. To do so, comparing it with those previously mentioned is mandatory. That is to say, Table 5 compares our proposal with MITRE

Table 5. Comparison of our proposal with MITRE ATT&CK

	Discovery	Exploitation	Inside	Pivoting	Logic
TA0043	X				
TA0042		X			
TA0001	X				
TA0002		X			
TA0003			X		
TA0004		X			
TA0005					X
TA0006			X		
TA0007	X			X	
TA0008				X	X
TA0009			X		
TA0011					X
TA0010			X		
TA0040		X	X		

Table 6. Comparison of our proposal with CKC

	Discovery	Exploitation	Inside	Pivoting	Logic
Reconnaissance	X				
Weaponization					X
Delivery		X	X	X	X
Exploitation		X			X
Installation			X		
Command and Control					X
Actions on Objective			X		

Table 7. Comparison of our proposal with HackTricks

	Discovery	Exploitation	Inside	Pivoting	Logic
Discovering	X				
Internal Test	X				
Port scan	X				
Searching service	X				
Pentesting service		X			
Phishing		X			
Getting shell		X			
Inside			X		
Exfiltration			X		
Privilege escalation			X		
Post			X		
Pivoting				X	

ATT&CK, while Table 6 contrasts it with CKC, and finally Table 7 compares it with HackTricks.

As depicted in these tables, for every stage of the matrix being compared, there is always one of the columns marked, i.e., all phases are included in the designed methodology, thus indicating that the novel matrix is complete. This means that sections of previous methodologies are compacted and oriented to automation, and the information in the other matrices is maintained, converging in a realistic attack methodology. That is, using this approach provides a solution to the question 1.

3.2 Logic Phase

The phases described above are correctly measured and compared with the other methodologies, demonstrating the capabilities of the Logic phase. In particular, the proposed methodology need a logic that controls and coheres the different phases for realistic attacks. It is worth remarking that we were inspired by the Observe, Orient, Decide, Act (OODA) loop [16]. The logic followed to concatenate the different phases is depicted in Fig. 1.

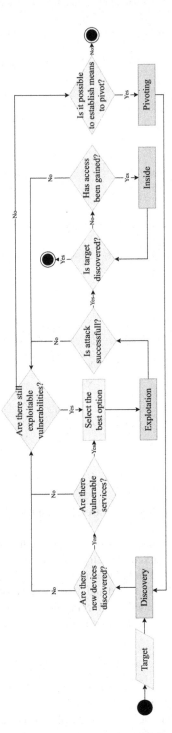

Fig. 1. Attack flowchart representing the phases of the proposed methodology within the Logic phase

The methodology followed starts with a "target". This is the application's objective and will determine the means of one of the two stop conditions. Once the agent starts, it tries to discover vulnerable equipment and their respective services, which implies the *Discovery* phase and use of tools like Nmap, an open source utility for network discovery and security auditing [17]. Next, it selects the best of the attack vectors, as explained in Sect. 3.2, and exploits them, which implies the *Exploitation* phase and uses tools like Metasploit, a penetration testing framework [18]. If the attack is successful, we will check if we have reached the target. If the target has been reached, the program terminates. Otherwise, we check if the attack gains access, a new agent will be deployed, and all the information of the new user machine is exfiltrated, which implies the *Inside* phase and use of its tool, like PEASS-ng, a privilege escalation tool and exfiltration [19]. Then it is checked again whether the target has been reached. If it has not been reached, we will check if "Has access been gained?" forcing the answer to be negative. Finally, the logic checks if there are additional vulnerabilities to exploit and repeats the process.

If, in any of the above decisions, we are unable to continue, we will go on to evaluate if there are any vulnerabilities left to exploit. Note that if we do not find any device after running the phase *Discovery* for the first time, we proceed to search for any remaining vulnerabilities. This decision is made because the agent has found vulnerabilities within the equipment where it is located.

Finally, the agents will perform the lateral movement if no vulnerabilities are left to exploit. This action involves the *Pivoting* phase and its tools. This phase is the last of the possibilities because this action implies a huge interaction with the network and is potentially detectable by Intrusion Detection Systems (IDS). If it is impossible to perform lateral movement on any of the computers, the attack will end.

The decisions made by the proposed logic also consider factors when the different phases take place, as we will see next.

Topology Exploration. At the time of the initial discovery of devices and vulnerabilities, or after the lateral movement, agents must consider which devices to analyze or attack. When it comes to decision-making in terms of cybersecurity, the experts in the field will be the ones to provide the basis. Depending on the objective the attacker is trying to achieve, we can categorize the attacks into various types, such as taking control of the machine, performing a denial of service on the victim organization, or stealing critical data, among others. Choosing one machine or another as a target in the "Discovery" phase will be determined by the initialization data, located in "Target".

To ensure a comprehensive network exploration, finding an algorithm that can achieve this goal is crucial. We have chosen the Breadth First Search (BFS) approach for our proposal, as it offers distinct advantages [20]. One of the significant benefits is that APTs can conduct this exploration in parallel, as illustrated in Fig. 2.

By distributing the exploration of the devices, the algorithm can scan the topology more efficiently, reducing the total search time. In addition, the parallel version of BFS maintains its sequential counterpart's completeness and optimality properties, guaranteeing that if there is a path from the outside to the target, BFS will find it because it is complete if the branching factor is finite. Since the topology is a graph of equally

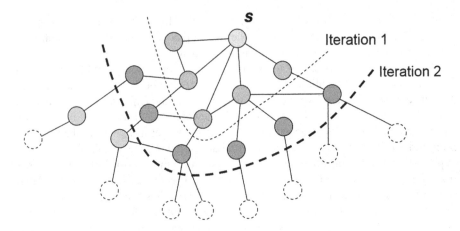

Fig. 2. Parallel breadth-first search of APTs for Discovery and Pivoting phases

weighted edges, it will find the shortest path eventually because if every node has the same cost, BFS is optimal. However, BSF's parallel feature must be used thoroughly to enhance IDS detection.

Select the Best Option. The *Explotation* phase is very extensive, since there are many and very heterogeneous vulnerabilities and possible offensive tools. Thanks to the architecture proposed in Sect. 4, the implementation of the phase will be able to couple tools used by professionals to the proposed methodology. The critical point in the proposed flow comes when it is necessary to decide which of the available attacks given by the supported tools will be executed. To solve this decision-making, a knowledge base is proposed where the "score" of the attack is stored and updated for each implemented tool. This option has been chosen for the following reasons: i) vulnerabilities are not always exploitable, ii) different interface implementations exist, depending on the tools used, and iii) the criticality is not always sufficient; priority should be given to attacks that enable the takeover of the equipment. In addition, exploitation depends on temporal, contextual, and even external factors, such as the stability of the network, among others. In Fig. 3, the knowledge base is denoted with red color, and is referred to as *Attack score*. After implementing the methodology and providing sufficient training time, the accuracy of vector exploitation will be improved. This will help in avoiding patched attack vectors. The Eq. 1 updates and stores the results, which helps in learning the best vectors to exploit.

$$score = (old\_score * n + CVSS * success\_lvl)/(n + 1) \tag{1}$$

where the variables take values depending on the following:

- *score*: The calculated gravity score. It will be stored in the knowledge base.
- *old_score*: The average score previously saved in the knowledge base and based on which it will be decided whether to use that attack vector.

- *n*: The number of times the average has been calculated.
- *CVSS*: Common Vulnerability Scoring System (CVSS) or criticality level of the detected vulnerability as determined by Forum of Incident Response and Security Teams.
- *success_lvl*: A variable that can take the values:
  - 0.2, being unable to exploit the vulnerability.
  - 1, when it is possible to exploit it and achieve the desired target or Remote Code Execution with a user who does not have root permissions.
  - 2, when exploit achieves Remote Code Execution with a user with root permissions.

The values used in the success level variable are a first approximation since they have desirable characteristics. For vulnerabilities patched to have a lower value, a value of 0.2 has been assigned to penalize this type of event. On the other hand, if the vulnerability has been successfully exploited, then we will speak of a factor of 1 since, as this value is the idempotence of the multiplication, it is equivalent not to punishing or rewarding the score. Finally, suppose that vulnerability returns a better result than expected, such as a user with administrator privileges. In that case, we will discuss a factor of 2 to promote using that vulnerability in future cases.

After an attempt to breach a system, the result will be stored, and the following data will be updated in the knowledge base: *score*, *glscvss*, and *n*. In case that attack has not obtained any result, the value of the success level variable will be one-fifth of the criticality value or *CVSS*, it will be registered in *Logic* and the next most promising one for a certain machine will be tested. The attacks start with the valuation established in *CVSS*, so if there is no record in the knowledge base, this value will be taken to make the comparison with the other available attacks.

The CVSS provides a standardized measure of the inherent severity of computer system vulnerabilities. However, it falls short as a sole metric for assessing their criticality due to its static nature and lack of contextual consideration. CVSS scores do not usually account for real-world factors such as the effectiveness of patches, mitigations, or the specific environmental conditions that affect exploitability, which can be added only with a quite deep knowledge of the network assets. This limitation underscores the need for a more comprehensive approach integrating dynamic, context-specific factors alongside CVSS scores. This formula aims to fix the problems that CVSS scores may expose in our context (i.e., simulation of APTs in a CR ecosystem), rewarding and punishing the attack vectors by experimenting with them.

By implementing a logical framework, we ensure that each process phase is distinct and interconnected, creating a coherent and comprehensive system. This approach, driven by logic, prevents stagnation from overly formulaic processes. Instead of adhering to a rigid structure, the system dynamically adjusts to various scenarios, maintaining unpredictability and adaptability. This adaptability is crucial for maintaining a sense of realism, as it mirrors the complexity and variability of real-world situations. The process remains relevant, engaging, and effective, avoiding over-simplification and embracing complexity. Furthermore, this logical integration promotes a deeper understanding and a more nuanced approach to problem-solving, as it requires and fosters an environment where critical thinking and innovation are paramount. In essence, logic is not just a tool for coherence but a catalyst for creativity and realism needed in a Cyber Range environment. Therefore, the training of people is effectively improved with automated network agents, and the propose stands that question 2 has been resolved.

4 Architecture

In this section, an architecture is proposed for carrying out the methodology. As previously mentioned, APT generators are proposed in this case, given their great power and importance in Cyber Ranges. The primary reason for selecting APTs is that they are globally regarded as the most challenging and relentless attacks. An additional abstraction layer is necessary for the proposal to implement the proposed matrix correctly. That is why we have resorted to creating an Application Programming Interface (API), which achieves homogeneity using different APT generators. Such an API interface will allow the methodology implementation to easily couple the tools used to perform real attacks, thus providing the methodology with the necessary realism in Cyber Range environments.

Furthermore, an API has been proposed for each stage, as various automation tools are available for exploiting vulnerabilities or security flaws. Within each API, the option to launch commands manually is also included because an instructor could control phases manually if needed. Streamlined integration is achieved through the use of it, facilitating seamless communication between various software applications and enhancing interoperability. Additionally, APIs allow systems to scale and adapt to new features or changes without requiring extensive modifications. The architecture is shown below in Fig. 3.

Specifically, differentiation between various components is based on their respective colors in figure above: i) *purple*, which houses the logic of each phase, intercommunicating the different tools and functionalities available; ii) *light blue*, which represents the interfaces corresponding to each stage of the methodology; iii) *orange*, which refers to the implementation of the interface for each available tool and a manual command launcher; iv) *gray*, which highlights each of the available tools; v) *red*, which represents where the knowledge base of the attacks is located; vi) and *green*, which houses how the API communicates with the APTs controller, specifically with the *Logic* class.

To run a complete implementation of the architecture, it will be necessary to have at least one tool implementing each interface. Otherwise, it will not be possible to loop over the methodology. An example of tool per phase would be: i) Nmap, a penetration testing framework as a *Discovery_tool* [17]; ii) Metasploit, a open source utility for network discovery and security auditing as an *Exploitation_tool* [18]; iii) PEASS-ng, a privilege escalation tool and exfiltration as an *Inside_tool* [19]; iv) SSHUTTLE, a VPN simulator over SSH connections as a *Pivoting_tool* [21]; v) CALDERA, an automated adversary emulation platform manager as *APT_controller* [22].

The solution's foundation lies in the interface *APT_controller*, which communicates the APTs of an existing tool with the rest of the architecture. In addition, *Logic* is in charge of intercommunicating and coordinating the rest of the phases, which is why the rest of the stages are contained in it.

The architecture's modular design offers numerous benefits. Each tool functions as a separate unit, minimizing the risk of systemic failure due to a single tool malfunction.

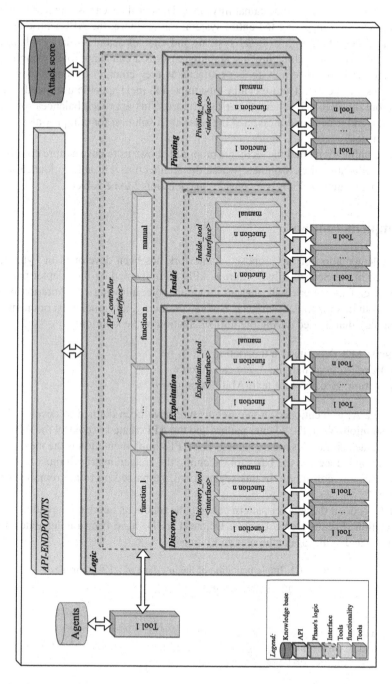

Fig. 3. An abstract overview of the proposed framework, highlighting the main components and phases

This separation enhances maintainability, as updates or fixes can be applied to individual tools without impacting the entire system. Furthermore, the API-centric approach facilitates integration with external systems and enables seamless data exchange and interoperability. The architecture's scalability ensures it can adapt to evolving requirements and accommodate new tools or attacks as they emerge. By embracing a user-centric design, the architecture can be customized to meet specific user needs, providing a more intuitive and efficient user experience. This approach balances robustness, flexibility, and user-friendliness, making it an ideal solution for complex and dynamic environments.

The combination of all the elements proposed allows us to have a more complex and complete educational environment where the architecture will able to launch realistic and automatic attacks. Thus, we consider the question 2 to be solved.

5   Implementation

The implementation of the proposed framework has been developed in Python, and, as defined in the Sect. 4, it has different APIs accompanied by the adapter pattern for each phase. This pattern will play an important role, allowing collaboration between objects with incompatible interfaces. Before continuing, it is crucial to comment on the terminology that is used during the implementation of the solution:

- **Agent**: APT deposited on the victim.
- **Abilities**: Actions that the *Agent* can execute.
- **Operation**: Execution of textitAbilities on *Agent*.

All the APIs mentioned in the architecture have been defined to develop the presented solution. Next, the adapter pattern and the API created to control the APT generators or attack simulators are explained. The API's implementation is the most complex and important since it is the basis for executing the created matrix. It must be carefully designed as any constraints in this segment will be passed on to the remainder of the solution.

In the code of the adapter pattern created, the functions of creation, reading, update, and deletion (Create, Read, Update, Delete, CRUD) have been implemented for the operations and skills, as can be seen in Listing 1.1:

Listing 1.1. Implementation of the interface of APT_controller

```
1 class APT_controller(Singleton):
2
3     #AGENTS
4     interface retrieve_agents()
5     interface retrieve_agent_detail(id)
6     interface delete_agent(id)
7
8     #ABILITIES
9     interface retrieve_abilities()
10    interface retrieve_abilities_by_tactic(id)
```

```
11      interface retrieve_abilities_by_tactic_string(id)
12      interface retrieve_ability_details(id)
13      interface add_ability(ability)
14      interface delete_abilities(ids)
15
16      #OPERATIONS
17      interface retrieve_operations()
18      interface retrieve_operation_details(id)
19      interface add_operation(operation)
20      interface delete_operation(id)
21      interface add_action_to_operation(ability)
```

The interfaces define methods that will later be redefined by the child classes, where the specific functionality of each tool will be implemented. In addition, the class uses the Singleton pattern to ensure that a class has only one instance, while providing a global access point to this instance.

Since the tool aims to extend and concatenate tools and functionalities, part of the implementation of the APT_controller's interface will developed to control, for example, Caldera. It will be shown below, specifically, the *Agents* and *Abilities* units as shown in Listing 1.2.

Listing 1.2. Implementation of the Caldera API 1/2

```
1 class Caldera(APT_controller):
2     def __init__(self, network_address):
3         self.api = Caldera_API(network_address)
4
5     #AGENTS
6     def retrieve_agents(self):
7         return self.api.get_agents()
8
9     def retrieve_agent_detail(self, id):
10        return self.api.get_agent_detail(id)
11
12    def delete_agent(self, ids):
13        return self.api.delete_agents(ids)
14
15    #ABILITIES
16    def retrieve_abilities(self):
17        return self.api.get_abilities()
18
19    def retrieve_abilities_by_tactic(self, id):
20        return self.format(self.api.get_abilities_by_tactic(id
                ))
21
22    def retrieve_abilities_by_tactic_string(self, id):
23        return self.format(self.api.
                get_abilities_by_tactic_string(id))
24
25    def retrieve_ability_details(self, id):
```

```
26            return self.api.get_ability_detail(id)
27
28    def add_ability(self, ability):
29            return self.api.add_ability(ability)
30    def delete_abilities(self, ids):
31
32            return self.api.delete_abilities(ids)
```

Some tools have their APIs, which operate through HTTP requests. It might be a good decision to create an additional class that encapsulates the "raw" API calls, like Caldera. This decision should be based on the repeated inconsistencies contained in the native API to solve future changes easily. Additionally, the control of the different responses and errors can be seen in Listing 1.3.

Listing 1.3. Implementation of the Caldera API 2/2

```
1 class Tool_API():
2     TOKEN = 'caldera_api_token'
3
4     Caldera_API(addr):
5         API_HTTP = connect(addr, token)
6
7     #AGENTS
8     function get_agents():
9         return API_HTTP.get('api/v2/agents')
10
11    funcion get_agents(agent):
12         return API_HTTP.get('api/v2/agents', agent)
13
14    funcion remove_agents(ids):
15         return API_HTTP.post('api/v2/agents', ids)
16
17    #ABILITIES
18    funcion get_abilities():
19         return API_HTTP.get('api/v2/abilities')
20
21    funcion get_abilities(id):
22         return API_HTTP.get('api/v2/abilities', id)
23
24    funcion add_ability(ability):
25         return API_HTTP.put('api/v2/abilities', ability)
26
27    funcion delete_abilitiy(id):
28         return API_HTTP.delete('api/v2/abilities', id)
```

In this last case, the utilization of CRUD methods is observed: i) creation, where objects are created (set); ii) reading, where objects are retrieved (get), iii) update, where objects are overwritten; iv) and delete, where objects are deleted (delete). In order to access the tool API, we use a token and the methods described in the documentation.

It is thanks to the union of both design decisions that the proposed solution can be independent of tools, avoid the drawbacks that it contains, and automate the attack methodology. Thus, we affirm that an APT simulator can be sufficiently autonomous and, above all, realistic. It would greatly enrich the experience of the student and will be able to better develop potential skills. Thus, the question 3 is considered solved.

6   Conclusions

Cybersecurity in healthcare safeguards sensitive patient data prevents identity theft, and ensures uninterrupted medical services. Breaches can compromise patient safety, disrupt operations, and erode trust in healthcare institutions. Robust security is vital for patient protection and maintaining healthcare integrity. To this end, it is essential to train users of computer systems with offensive and defensive skills. Cyber Ranges have proven to be a crucial tool for the latter, hosting realistic attack agents to train users automatically.

To better argue on the current and future capabilities of the automatic attack frameworks within the Cyber Range ecosystem, we have raised three research questions in this article, which we have demonstrated and answered affirmatively throughout the text. In particular, we believe that APT simulators can follow realistic attack matrices thanks to the proposed matrix. Then, the proposed matrix is sufficiently autonomous to perform an attack due to the methodology proposed. Finally, because of realism, APT simulators are useful to Cyber Range users to improve their cybersecurity skills.

In this context, our proposal's primary motivation stems from current attack matrices' inability to be oriented towards adaptive and realistic automation of attacks in Cyber Ranges environments. This is why a matrix was developed, generalizing enough to encompass all the necessary concepts and avoid losing information or utility. From it, we have developed an architecture where tools are implemented per stage that, in a modular way, can host the functionality required by the methodology. APIs enable seamless integration and communication between diverse tool implementations, promoting scalability, efficiency, and innovation. They facilitate rapid development, enhance security through controlled access, and extend reach and flexibility in the landscape.

Although the contribution has a huge potential, it requires further refinement for upcoming endeavors. We will continue to investigate different options and the challenges that lie ahead in Cyber Ranges environments. Ideally, a micro-service tailored to utilize within a Cyber Range should be implemented to test compatibility with other modules. Moreover, we aim to explore techniques suggesting realistic waiting periods shaped by fluctuating challenges while ensuring student engagement. Alongside this, we are looking into the infusion of artificial intelligence to supplant some functionality located on *Logic*, as the selection of the best option exploiting vulnerabilities, ushering in a deeper layer of authenticity.

Acknowledgments. This work has been partially funded by the Spanish Ministry of Universities linked to the European Union through the NextGenerationEU programme, from the postdoctoral grant Margarita Salas (172/MSJD/22), and from the strategic project CDL-TALENTUM from the Spanish National Institute of Cybersecurity (INCIBE) and by the Recovery, Transformation and Resilience Plan, NextGenerationEU. Authors acknowledge as well support from the CybAlliance project (Grant no. 337316).

References

1. Viewpoint: For stronger tech, Europe must spend more on defence and research. https://sciencebusiness.net/viewpoint/Sovereignty/stronger-tech-europe-must-spend-more-defence-and-research. Accessed 20 Apr 2023
2. López Martínez, A., Gil Pérez, M., Ruiz-Martínez, A.: A comprehensive review of the state-of-the-art on security and privacy issues in healthcare. ACM Comput. Surv. **55**(12) (2023). https://doi.org/10.1145/3571156
3. Cavaliere, G.A., Alfalasi, R., Jasani, G.N., Ciottone, G.R., Lawner, B.J.: Terrorist attacks against healthcare facilities: a review. Health Secur. **19**(5), 546–550 (2021)
4. Newaz, A.I., Sikder, A.K., Rahman, M.A., Uluagac, A.S.: A survey on security and privacy issues in modern healthcare systems: attacks and defenses. ACM Trans. Comput. Healthc. **2**(3), 1–44 (2021)
5. Vishnu, S., Ramson, S.J., Jegan, R.: Internet of medical things (IoMT) - an overview. In: 2020 5th International Conference on Devices, Circuits and Systems (ICDCS), pp. 101–104 (2020)
6. Razaque, A., et al.: Survey: cybersecurity vulnerabilities, attacks and solutions in the medical domain. IEEE Access **7**, 168774–168797 (2019)
7. Fatima, A., et al.: Impact and research challenges of penetrating testing and vulnerability assessment on network threat. In: 2023 International Conference on Business Analytics for Technology and Security (ICBATS), pp. 1–8 (2023)
8. Vats, P., Mandot, M., Gosain, A.: A comprehensive literature review of penetration testing & its applications. In: 2020 8th International Conference on Reliability, Infocom Technologies and Optimization (Trends and Future Directions) (ICRITO), pp. 674–680 (2020)
9. Nespoli, P., Albaladejo-González, M., Pastor Valera, J.A., Ruipérez-Valiente, J.A., Gómez Mármol, F.: Capacidades avanzadas de simulación y evaluación con elementos de gamificación. In: VII Jornadas Nacionales de Investigación en Ciberseguridad (JNIC 2022), pp. 55–62 (2022)
10. World Economic Forum: WEF global cybersecurity outlook 2022. World Economic Forum, Technical Report (2022). https://www3.weforum.org/docs/WEF_Global_Cybersecurity_Outlook_2022.pdf
11. Nespoli, P., Papamartzivanos, D., Gómez Mármol, F., Kambourakis, G.: Optimal counter-measures selection against cyber attacks: a comprehensive survey on reaction frameworks. IEEE Commun. Surv. Tutor. **20**(2), 1361–1396 (2018)
12. Stefinko, Y., Piskozub, A., Banakh, R.: Manual and automated penetration testing. Benefits and drawbacks. Modern tendency. In: 2016 13th International Conference on Modern Problems of Radio Engineering, Telecommunications and Computer Science (TCSET), pp. 488–491 (2016)
13. Xiong, W., Legrand, E., Åberg, O., Lagerström, R.: Cyber security threat modeling based on the MITRE enterprise ATT&CK matrix. Softw. Syst. Model. **21**(1), 157–177 (2022)
14. Yadav, T., Rao, A.M.: Technical aspects of cyber kill chain. In: Abawajy, J.H., Mukherjea, S., Thampi, S.M., Ruiz-Martínez, A. (eds.) SSCC 2015. CCIS, vol. 536, pp. 438–452. Springer, Cham (2015). https://doi.org/10.1007/978-3-319-22915-7_40
15. Castaño, C.P.: Hacktricks. https://book.hacktricks.xyz/welcome/readme. Accessed 26 Apr 2023
16. Richards, C.: Boyd's ooda loop (2020)
17. Lyon, G.F.: Nmap Network Scanning: The Official Nmap Project Guide to Network Discovery and Security Scanning. Insecure, Sunnyvale (2009)
18. Kennedy, D., O'Gorman, J., Kearns, D., Aharoni, M.: Metasploit: The Penetration Tester's Guide, 1st edn. No Starch Press, USA (2011)

19. Polop, C.: Peass-ng (2023). https://github.com/carlospolop/PEASS-ng
20. Kurant, M., Markopoulou, A., Thiran, P.: On the bias of BFS (breadth first search). In: 2010 22nd International Teletraffic Congress (lTC 22), pp. 1–8 (2010)
21. sshuttle: Sshuttle (2023). https://github.com/sshuttle/sshuttle
22. Alford, R., Lawrence, D., Kouremetis, M.: Caldera: a red-blue cyber operations automation platform. In: Proceedings of the 32nd International Conference on Automated Planning and Scheduling, 13–24 June 2022 (2022)

Author Index

Printed in the United States
by Baker & Taylor Publisher Services